Myanmar's Foreign Exchange Market

Koji Kubo

Myanmar's Foreign Exchange Market

Controls, Reforms, and Informal Market

Springer

Koji Kubo
Institute of Developing Economies,
Japan External Trade Organization
(IDE-JETRO)
Chiba, Japan

ISBN 978-981-13-1788-0 ISBN 978-981-13-1789-7 (eBook)
https://doi.org/10.1007/978-981-13-1789-7

Library of Congress Control Number: 2018950943

This Springer imprint is published by the registered company Springer Nature Singapore Pte Ltd.
The registered company address is: 152 Beach Road, #21-01/04 Gateway East, Singapore 189721, Singapore

Preface

This book presents a bird's-eye view of Myanmar's foreign exchange market in the past and present. Until now, the country's foreign exchange market has been shrouded in mystery. In the past, authorities implemented a wide range of arbitrary regulations and controls on international trade and foreign exchange, which spurred a myriad of informal economic activities including informal currency deals, smuggling, and international money transfer outside banks. The official exchange rate, which was pegged to the special drawing rights of the International Monetary Fund (IMF), remained at around 6 kyats per U.S. dollar, whereas the prevailing unofficial market rate fluctuated above 1300 kyats per U.S. dollar in the late 2000s. This was one of the worst disparities between the official and unofficial market rates at that time. It was not clear how the official foreign exchange regime was implemented on the one hand and how the unofficial foreign exchange market functioned on the other.

Despite the foreign exchange policy reform with the IMF's technical assistance since 2011, Myanmar's foreign exchange market has preserved features of its pre-reform period such as prevalent informal currency deals outside banks. The small turnover of interbank foreign currency deals suggests that the official market institution remains weak. The evolution of the foreign exchange market exhibits path dependence.

Given that path dependence, the chronology and overview of the foreign exchange market that this book provides will be indispensable for understanding current phenomena in the market. The book is thus intended for policymakers confronting the unofficial foreign exchange market as well as for academics who are interested in Myanmar's economy.

Based on my extensive fieldwork in Myanmar to complement the sparse literature on it, this volume unveils the structure of the country's foreign exchange market. I conducted numerous interviews with officials of state-owned and private banks and with financial authorities, as well as carrying out questionnaire surveys of private exporters and importers on their foreign currency transactions. I was stationed in Yangon, Myanmar's largest commercial city, for a long-term foreign residency research program of the Institute of Developing Economies, Japan

External Trade Organization (IDE-JETRO) for 2 years, from October 2006 to October 2008. It allowed me to acquire a rough picture of the unofficial foreign exchange market in the pre-reform period. Subsequently, I was assigned to a resident researcher position at JETRO's Bangkok office from April 2012 to July 2016, during which I made frequent visits to neighboring Myanmar for fieldwork. This coincided with a period when the foreign exchange policy reform gained its momentum, including exchange rate unification in April 2012. I would like to express my most profound gratitude to IDE-JETRO for the opportunities they gave me to research Myanmar's economy.

This book would not have been possible without several rounds of questionnaire surveys on the unofficial foreign exchange market in the pre- and post-reform periods, in which I gained first-hand information about Myanmar's private exporters and importers involved in informal currency deals. Aung Min, Phyo Kyaw Thu, and Kyaw Hlaing provided invaluable support for the surveys.

I am grateful to the officials and retired officials of the Central Bank of Myanmar, including Than Lwin, Winston Set Aung, Naw Eh Hpaw, Win Thaw, Min Han Soe, Khin Thida Maw, and Cho Cho Thein, who shared with me their views and ideas on the rapidly changing foreign exchange market during the reform period.

I am indebted to Masaru Tanaka and Shunsuke Yamamoto who assisted the foreign exchange market reform as advisors from inside the Central Bank of Myanmar. Their insights into Myanmar's economy from the point of view of regulators and bankers helped me to burnish my understanding of the country's foreign exchange market. Discussion on international banking and Myanmar's financial system with Satoshi Okagawa and Yasuhisa Ojima is also gratefully acknowledged.

Many thanks are due to Toshihiro Kudo, who introduced me to many resource persons in Myanmar. Shin'ichi Watanabe and Bhanupong Nidhiprabha provided support and encouragement for compiling my experiences and knowledge on Myanmar's economy in this book, which has been an overwhelming and enormous task. While there are not many scholars who share common interests in Myanmar's financial sector, I am particularly indebted to Fumiharu Mieno and Sean Turnell for discussions, as well as to their research. Last but not least, I would like to thank Tsunehiro Otsuki, Hiro Lee, Kozo Kunimune, and two anonymous reviewers for their insightful comments that significantly contributed to improving the manuscript.

Earlier versions of chapters in this book were published in the following journals: the *ASEAN Economic Review* (and its successor, the *Journal of Southeast Asian Economies*), *Asian-Pacific Economic Literature*, the *Global Economic Review*, and *Post-Communist Economies*. I express my gratitude to the respective publishers for their permission to reuse some content. I also gratefully acknowledge financial support from the Japan Society for the Promotion of Science through the Grant-in-Aid for Scientific Research (C) No. 26380352.

Chiba, Japan — Koji Kubo

Contents

About the Author

Koji Kubo is a Senior Research Fellow at the Institute of Developing Economies, Japan External Trade Organization (IDE-JETRO). Earlier drafts of this book were written, while he was affiliated with the JETRO Bangkok Office as a researcher and with the Institute of Asian Studies, Chulalongkorn University in Thailand as a visiting researcher. He has a Ph.D. in international public policy from Osaka University and degrees from Kyoto University and the University of Sussex.

His research focuses on the evolution of economic institutions in Myanmar. His analyses of the Myanmar economy have appeared in the *ASEAN Economic Bulletin*, *Asian-Pacific Economic Literature*, the *Journal of Southeast Asian Economies*, and *Post-Communist Economies*. He is the editor of *Dollarization and De-dollarization in Transitional Economies of Southeast Asia* (2017).

Abbreviations

AREAER	*Annual Report on Exchange Arrangements and Exchange Restrictions* of the International Monetary Fund
ASEAN	Association of Southeast Asian Nations
BIS	Bank for International Settlements
CBM	Central Bank of Myanmar
CPI	Consumer Price Index
DOTS	*Direction of Trade Statistics*
FCDs	Foreign Currency Deposits
FDI	Foreign Direct Investment
FECs	Foreign Exchange Certificates
FY	Fiscal Year
IMF	International Monetary Fund
MCP	Multiple Currency Practice
MEB	Myanma Economic Bank
MFTB	Myanma Foreign Trade Bank
MICB	Myanma Investment and Commercial Bank
MoFR	Ministry of Finance and Revenue
SDR	Special Drawing Rights
SEEs	State Economic Enterprises
SFA	State Fund Account
SMEI	*Selected Monthly Economic Indicators*

List of Figures

Chapter 4

Chapter 5

Chapter 6

List of Tables

Chapter 5

Chapter 6

Chapter 1
Introductory Chapter: Myanmar's Foreign Exchange Market—Controls, Reforms, and Informal Market

Abstract Under extensive controls on foreign exchange and international trade, Myanmar's foreign exchange market has achieved its development which is characterized by the prevalent informal currency deals. Clarifying how Myanmar has diverted from the premises of the existing policy analyses, we unveil the evolution and functions of its foreign exchange market. Toward this goal, we introduce the concept of an informal interfirm-based market and contrast it with the conventional bank-based market model. By presenting the costs and benefits of informal currency deals, we discuss the rationale for the market reform in Myanmar. Furthermore, understanding the trajectory of the foreign exchange market serves as the basis for an investigation of the root causes of Myanmar's persistent informal currency deals in the post-exchange rate unification period. This analytical narrative contributes to the literature on foreign exchange policy reforms in developing countries.

Keywords Informal currency deal · Interfirm-based forex market
Bank-based forex market · Exchange restriction · Myanmar

1 Introduction

Foreign exchange policies in developing and transitional economies have drawn a large volume of research. In the extensive body of literature on foreign exchange (forex) markets, researchers studied issues such as exchange rate regime choices (Williamson 2000; Fischer 2001; Ghosh et al. 2002) and capital account convertibility (Kenen 1998; Ariyoshi et al. 2000; Eichengreen 2001; Henry 2007).

While pertinent, a relatively less studied issue is the forex market organization and its evolution in developing and transitional economies. Lyons (2001) provides a seminal work on the microstructure approach to the forex market. Touching on the market organization, however, his works and other studies that followed mostly focus on the determination of exchange rates.

Scarce attention to the forex market organization in the literature might be because of the presumption that the forex market is a bank-based organization. Studies of the

K. Kubo, *Myanmar's Foreign Exchange Market*,
https://doi.org/10.1007/978-981-13-1789-7_1

forex market organization in developing economies by the International Monetary Fund (IMF) (1999, 2003) fall in this line. From this perspective, easing restrictions on banks' activities ensures the development of the forex market. Lifting exchange restrictions facilitates banks to trade foreign exchange actively, enhancing market liquidity. A sound banking sector is conducive to forex market sophistication in financial derivative dealing, which enables market participants to manage exchange rate risk.

Likewise, concerning foreign exchange policy reforms in countries that experienced multiple exchange rates, structural changes in the forex market organization after lifting exchange restrictions are rarely studied.[1] In a survey of unofficial forex markets in eight developing countries by Kiguel and O'Connell (1995), exchange rate unification and the dissolution of unofficial forex markets are understood as two sides of a coin, taking place simultaneously. Lifting exchange restrictions is considered sufficient both to unify exchange rates and to eliminate informal currency deals. Perhaps this is due to the presumption of higher transaction costs in the unofficial market relative to those in the official market; when underlying exchange restrictions, such as import bans that motivate residents in informal currency deals, are eased, there is no longer a reason to continue the costly informal deals. From this perspective, lifting exchange restrictions would ensure banks to absorb informal currency deals.

A puzzling phenomenon in Myanmar is that informal currency deals remain pervasive, although the country has embarked on holistic forex market reforms since 2011 and mostly succeeded in exchange rate unification. To address this puzzle, we loosen the assumption that the forex market is bank-based. While informal currency deals are common in developing and transitional countries (Reinhart and Rogoff 2004), the prevalence of informal currency deals in Myanmar must be of a different order from most. Dismissing the premise of a bank-based forex market, we introduce the concept of the informal interfirm-based forex market, in which informal currency deals between non-financial firms overwhelm official currency deals at banks.

This book focuses on the evolution of the forex market organization in Myanmar. Existing studies on Myanmar are rather confined to analyzing the distortionary effects of multiple exchange rates,[2] such as in Myat Thein (2004), Turnell (2009, 2011), and Hori and Wong (2013). By contrast, we explore the evolution of the forex market organization and investigate the persistence of informal currency deals during the reform period.

We explore Myanmar's forex market in the following order. First, by assessing the administrative controls on foreign exchange and international trade during the 1988–2011 period, Chaps. 2–4 trace the emergence of what we call the informal interfirm-based forex market and its functions. Chapter 5 illustrates the foreign

[1] The exceptions are studies on the evolution of forex markets in transitional economies, including those on China (Mehran et al. 1996; Ding 1998) and Vietnam (Nguyen and Nguyen 2009).

[2] Apart from these studies, various issues of the IMF's Staff Reports for the Article IV Consultations provide useful descriptions of foreign exchange regulatory changes for each year. However, they lack historical backgrounds or require readers to have prior knowledge to fully comprehend the arguments.

exchange policy reforms since 2011 and evaluates the extent of integration between the new official market and the unofficial market. Chapter 6 diagnoses the persistent informal currency deals in the reform period using a quantitative analysis of the survey data of private firms. Chapter 7 summarizes the findings and offers prospects for the modernization of the forex market in Myanmar.

The novelty of this book is its examination of the evolution of the unofficial forex market. Among what Collier (2007) labels fragile states, where the government has weak capacity to implement regulations, some appear burdened with the informal interfirm-based forex market as in Myanmar. Lessons learned from the experience of Myanmar might have implications for them. Other fragile states go beyond Myanmar into a high magnitude of de facto dollarization as in Cambodia, where foreign currencies substitute for the local currency as a medium of exchange, a unit of account, and a store of value. Although dollarization is also observable to some extent in Myanmar, we do not cover it in this book and leave it to Kubo (2017) to streamline the analysis.

The remainder of this introductory chapter is structured as follows. Sections 2 and 3 analytically describe the backdrop of the research question, drawing on the review of the related literature and some statistics about the forex market organization. In particular, using the forerunners of the Association of Southeast Asian Nations (ASEAN) as a yardstick, Sect. 2 illustrates the benchmark structure and evolution of a bank-based forex market. Section 3 characterizes the unofficial forex market in contrast to the official bank-based market. Section 4 frames the research question and states the rationale for addressing this question. Section 5 presents the plan of this book.

2 Bank-Based Forex Market

To accentuate the peculiar feature of Myanmar's forex market structure, we illustrate a benchmark forex market structure common in emerging and industrialized countries, which we label a bank-based forex market. First, we describe the structure of a bank-based forex market and then show a typical trajectory of its evolution.

2.1 Market Structure

A common form of the forex market in emerging and industrialized countries is a dealer market in which interdealer (interbank) trading serves as the hub that integrates the market. With a particular focus on the roles of authorized dealers (banks), we illustrate a typical structure of a dealer market. We use the terms "bank-based market" and "dealer market" interchangeably.

2.1.1 Benchmark Dealer Market

Drawing on Lyons (2001: 41), we describe a generic form of a dealer market. We categorize players in a dealer market into three parties:

(1) Dealers
(2) Customers (including the central bank)
(3) Brokers

The first group, dealers, are licensed by authorities to trade foreign exchange among them and with customers (clients). Banks are commonly licensed as foreign exchange dealers. When requested by customers and other dealers, they present both the buying and selling prices of foreign exchange. The second group, customers, includes exporters and importers, individuals, and financial institutions such as pension funds. Customers do not trade foreign exchange between them. Their counterparties of currency deals are dealers. In the third group, brokers (voice brokers), collect buying and selling orders from dealers and match them, taking commissions. They do not buy or sell foreign exchange on their own accounts.

Another important player is the central bank. The central bank's foreign exchange interventions are usually market-based; it approaches major dealers to buy or sell foreign exchange for market interventions. In this regard, we classify the central bank as a customer.

There are two types of foreign currency deals in a dealer market:

(1) Interdealer trading
(2) Customer dealing

Interdealer trading includes wholesale transactions between dealers, where they adjust foreign exchange positions. Customer dealing is retail transactions between a dealer and a customer.

Interdealer trading can be further divided into (i) a direct interdealer trade and (ii) a brokered interdealer trade. In a direct interdealer trade, dealers communicate buying (bid) and selling (offer) prices of foreign exchange with each other, disclosing their identities to counterparties. By contrast, in a brokered interdealer trade, dealers post bids and offers on electronic trading platforms or on voice brokers that match buyers and sellers. While it requires some commission fees, brokered trade enables dealers to gain information about the market conditions[3] and price quotes without disclosing their identities to sellers.

In customer dealing, dealers present bid and offer prices to customers, who decide whether to take them or leave them. Dealers maintain foreign exchange liquidity on hand to accommodate orders from customers immediately. Immediacy is the service that dealers provide in customer dealing. The spread (bid–ask spread)—the gap

[3]Instead of quoting specific prices, dealers may place limit orders and market orders to brokers. Limit orders are conditional orders that a dealer buys or sells foreign exchange when the market reaches a specified price. Market orders are to buy or sell foreign exchange at the best available price. These allow dealers to gain the information about market conditions from brokers.

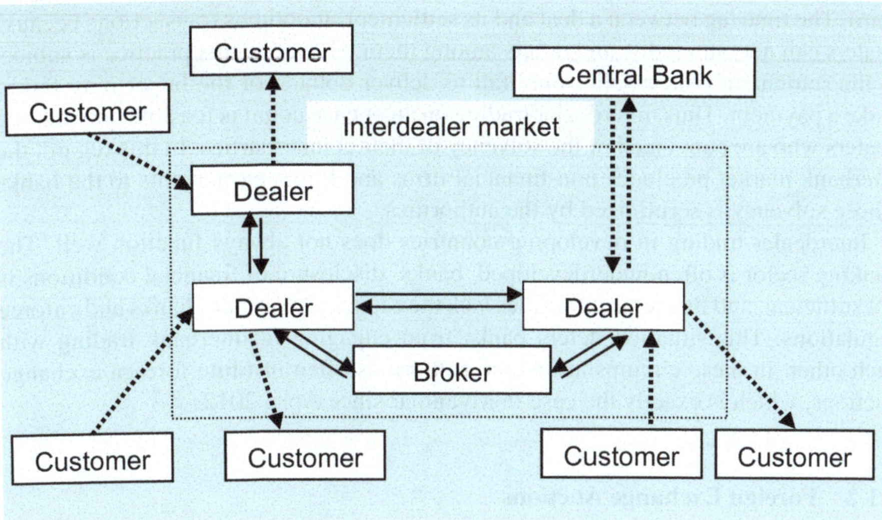

Fig. 1 A generic foreign exchange dealer market. *Source* Author

between the buy and sell prices of foreign exchange—is wider in customer dealing than in interdealer trading, which is the compensation for the immediacy service.

Interdealer trading integrates the otherwise fragmented forex market. A dealer market is decentralized by nature; multiple deals take place concurrently at different prices. Figure 1 depicts a generic form of a dealer market. In this figure, arrows with continuous lines refer to interdealer trading, and those with dotted lines refer to customer dealing. The figure shows deliberately that all market participants—dealers, customers, and brokers—are connected through interdealer trading. This link facilitates dealers to arbitrage between deals, which levels out exchange rates in the decentralized market.

A concentration of foreign exchange trades in dealers adds to market liquidity. Liquidity refers to the market's readiness to accommodate deals, and it is conducive to exchange rate stability. The IMF (1999) states that liquidity emerges when the market reaches a critical mass in terms of numbers of participants and transactions. It further states that "market liquidity can be seen as a form of positive externality or public goods, providing benefits to all actual or potential users of the market" (IMF 1999: 113). Intuitively, as dealers handle an increasing amount of both selling and buying orders, they can expand the currency trading turnover with the same size of liquidity at hand, which helps lower transaction costs. Furthermore, as order flows from customers concentrate in them, dealers can predict exchange rates, act as price setters, and provide liquidity to the market.

For smooth interdealer trading among authorized dealer banks, financial authorities' bank supervision is indispensable. In the interbank market, dealers trade foreign exchange on an open account; settlements of currency deals usually take place afterward. The time lag between a deal and its settlement smoothens transactions because dealers can net out credits and debits among them. However, this practice is subject to the settlement risk; a seller may fail to deliver dollars, or the buyer may fail to make a payment. Thus, interdealer trading on an open account is feasible only among dealers who are convinced of the solvency of their counterparties. In this regard, the interbank market precludes non-financial firms and limits participants to the banks whose solvency is scrutinized by the authorities.

Interdealer trading in developing countries does not always function well. The banking sector is often underdeveloped, banks' disclosure of financial conditions is not sufficient, and financial authorities lack the capacity to monitor banks and enforce regulations. This situation deters banks from engaging in interbank trading with each other. In these circumstances, the authorities often institute foreign exchange auctions, which is exactly the case in Myanmar since April 2012.

2.1.2 Foreign Exchange Auctions

In developing countries where interdealer trading is in an immature stage, financial authorities often substitute foreign exchange auctions for an interdealer market.[4] Foreign exchange auctions by financial authorities provide market liquidity and stabilize exchange rates.

For illustrative purpose, we describe a generic form of foreign exchange auctions. Auctions are one-sided, where the central bank sells foreign exchange to authorized dealer banks periodically—daily or once per week. With regard to sources of foreign exchange, the government channels the foreign exchange receipts from state enterprises, international aid, and foreign debts to the central bank, or it mandates exporters to surrender export proceeds to the central bank. At auctions, the central bank calls for bids from authorized dealer banks. The central bank sets the cut-off price, and the banks whose bids are above it are entitled to purchase foreign exchange. The central bank announces the cut-off rate of the auction as the official market exchange rate. Obtaining foreign exchange in the auction, authorized dealer banks sell it to customers through customer dealing or to other banks through interdealer trading.

We emphasize that in a forex market with auctions, authorized dealer banks are still the primary agents that channel foreign exchange to non-financial firms, as in the forex market with interdealer trading. While auctions substitute for interdealer trading, its market structure is regarded as bank-based.

[4]IMF (2003) classifies the interdealer trade using electronic trading platforms—the electronic brokered system (EBS) and the Reuters system—as an auction market. We categorize them as a dealer market.

2.2 *Market Evolution*

Drawing on the experiences of four ASEAN forerunners, Indonesia, Malaysia, the Philippines, and Thailand, we describe the evolution of the bank-based forex market. First, we argue that some key regulations shaped the bank-based forex market in these countries. Second, with the statistics on the forex market in these countries, we present how the forex market developed in terms of the content and size.

2.2.1 Exchange Rate Regimes and Regulatory Framework

While the IMF (2003) presumes a bank-based structure for any forex markets, we argue that its two main features, namely (i) the concentration of currency deals in banks and (ii) interdealer trading (interbank market) that integrates the market, are formed by exchange restrictions and are closely related with exchange rate regimes.

First, for the concentration of currency deals at banks, there are three crucial components of exchange restrictions:

(1) Surrender requirement
(2) Repatriation requirement
(3) Controls on foreign currency deposits

Among these three components, surrender and repatriation requirements are precisely documented in the IMF's *Annual Report on Exchange Arrangements and Exchange Restrictions* (AREAER).

We can contrast the surrender requirement and the repatriation requirement as follows. For the surrender requirement, authorities mandate exporters to sell export proceeds either to authorized dealer banks or the central bank, sometimes at the designated exchange rate. For the repatriation requirement, authorities mandate exporters to transfer export proceeds to the home country, not allowing them to maintain them at offshore bank accounts. Between these two controls, the surrender requirement is more restrictive than the repatriation requirement. In the regime with the repatriation requirement but no surrender requirement, exporters are permitted to maintain foreign currency deposits (FCDs) at banks in the home country; exporters repatriate export proceeds and keep them as dollar assets in banks of the home country, rather than selling them for the local currency.

Concerning the controls on FCDs, while their full accounts are not given in AREAER, they still influence the structure of the forex market. Prohibition of FCD transfers to other resident accounts is compatible with the bank-based forex market. If domestic account transfers of FCDs are prohibited, exporters would have no options but to dispose of FCDs in either their own international payments (imports) or sales to the bank where they deposit dollars. By contrast, tolerating domestic account transfers of FCDs would facilitate foreign exchange deals between non-financial firms. Domestic account transfers of FCDs are highly compatible with informal currency deals.

Prohibition of FCD withdrawal in foreign currency notes is similar but less crucial than prohibiting domestic account transfers. After withdrawal in foreign currency notes, depositors can convert them outside banks to the local currency. However, transactions using large amounts of foreign currency notes are cumbersome and costly because banks would impose handling charges on withdrawals and acceptance of foreign currency notes. Such transaction costs would deter informal foreign currency deals using cash.

The summary of the changes in the surrender and repatriation requirements in the ASEAN-4 forerunner countries in Table 1 shows that the surrender requirement was in place in all of these countries at the end of the Bretton Woods fixed exchange rate system in 1970. Later on, these countries gradually eased their exchange restrictions. The repatriation requirement was lifted in Indonesia and the Philippines. The surrender requirement was lifted in Indonesia, Malaysia, and the Philippines, but Malaysia temporarily reintroduced it in the aftermath of the 1997 Asian financial crisis. Thailand maintained the strictest exchange restrictions among the four countries, but its financial authorities recently allowed exporters to retain a part of export proceeds as FCDs within the ceiling that is determined in proportion to firms' export size.

We interpret this to mean that strict enforcement of the surrender requirement in earlier years ensured a concentration of currency deals at banks and marginalized currency deals between non-financial firms, providing the foundation of a bank-based forex market. While exchange restrictions were eased later on, banks remained the hub of the forex market.

Interdealer trading (interbank market) has come to play its role in these ASEAN forerunners since their shift to independently floating and managed floating in the aftermath of the Asian financial crisis in 1997. Before the collapse of the Bretton Woods fixed exchange rate system in March 1973, the authorities directed that banks allocate foreign exchange at the specified exchange rates. As McKinnon and Schnabl (2004), among others, argue, even after the collapse of the Bretton Woods system, these countries maintained their currency peg to the U.S. dollar. It was the 1997 Asian financial crisis that provided the spark for their move to the managed floating exchange rate regime.[5] Controls on exchange rates were eased, which led to the development of interdealer trading. The experiences of Indonesia, the Philippines, and Thailand fit the view of the IMF (2003) that easing restrictions on banks' activities is sufficient for the development of interdealer trading.

2.2.2 Spot Transactions versus Forward and Swap Contracts

Next, we illustrate the development of the forex market in the ASEAN-4 forerunner countries in quantitative terms. The data source is the *Triennial Central Bank Survey of Foreign Exchange and Derivative Market Activity* by the Bank for International Settlements (BIS). The survey is based on the reports by foreign exchange dealer

---

[5] Malaysia resumed to the de facto peg to the U.S. dollar afterward.

Table 1 Exchange restrictions in selected Southeast Asian countries

	AREAER year	Proceeds from exports and invisible transactions	
		Repatriation requirement	Surrender requirement
Myanmar	2000	Yes	No
	2008	Yes	No
Indonesia	1970	Yes	Surrender at the official exchange rate
	1980	Yes	To authorized banks
	1990	No	No
	2000	No	No
	2008	No	No
Malaysia	1970	Yes	To authorized banks
	1980	Yes	No
	1990	Yes	No
	2000	Yes	Limit $10 mil.
	2008	Yes	No
Philippines	1970	Yes	To authorized banks
	1980	Yes	To authorized banks
	1990	Yes	To authorized banks
	2000	No	No
	2008	No	No
Thailand	1970	Yes	To authorized banks
	1980	Yes	To authorized banks
	1990	Yes	To authorized banks
	2000	Yes	To authorized banks
	2008	Yes	Limit up to $2 mil.

Sources IMF AREAER (various issues)

banks in each country.[6] The BIS survey started in 1986 and every three years provides various statistics on forex market activities. The BIS survey has covered the ASEAN-4 countries since 1998.

One dimension of the development of the forex market is a shift from spot transactions to forward and swap contracts. Intuitively, forward is a financial contract that facilitates exporters and importers to hedge the exchange rate risk, while a swap is a contract for financial institutions to cover the exchange rate risk as well as to arbitrage between financial markets of different currencies (Luca 2000). These financial derivatives are indispensable in the modern forex market. By contrast, the bulk of

[6]The number of participating countries and regions in the 2016 survey is 52. Among the ASEAN members, Indonesia, Malaysia, the Philippines, Singapore, and Thailand participate in the survey.

the currency deals in underdeveloped forex markets, such as Vietnam's, are spot transactions (Nguyen and Nguyen 2009).

The summary of the daily average forex market turnover, and proportions of spot transactions and forward and swap contracts in Table 2 shows that the forex market turnover has been growing, though with some fluctuations, in all of these countries. For the period from 1998 through 2016, the turnover grew about threefold in Indonesia, the Philippines, and Thailand, and sevenfold in Malaysia. Furthermore, the table shows that a significant proportion of foreign exchange deals in these countries are forward and swap contracts rather than spot transactions.

We can also confirm that interdealer trading (interbank market) accounts for a sizable portion of the market turnover. Table 3 shows the forex market turnover by type of reporting dealers' counterparty as of April 2016. Counterparties are classified as (i) another local dealer, (ii) a dealer abroad, (iii) other financial institutions, and (iv) non-financial customers. In the terminology of the previous subsection, (i) and (ii) represent interdealer trading, and (iii) and (iv) are customer dealing. Among customer dealing, (iii) includes hedge funds and institutional investors, and (iv) includes exporters and importers for current international transactions. From this table, it is evident that non-financial customers—currency deals pertinent to current international transactions—account for a relatively minor portion of the market turnover, between 10.9 and 21.2% in these countries. In fact, the market turnover is higher

Table 2 Foreign exchange market turnover and types of transactions in selected Southeast Asian countries

Year	1998	2001	2004	2007	2010	2013	2016
Turnover (daily averages in April): US dollar, million							
Indonesia	1,766	3,875	2,332	3,039	3,381	5,011	4,633
Malaysia	1,143	1,362	1,653	3,482	7,147	11,095	8,361
Philippines	759	1,064	678	2,338	5,017	3,733	2,578
Thailand	3,119	1,912	3,119	6,314	7,390	12,784	10,544
Spot transactions: % of turnover							
Indonesia	41.3	86.2	41.9	55.4	64.6	66.8	52.2
Malaysia	30.0	34.3	48.3	48.0	54.8	45.2	18.4
Philippines	46.9	43.1	50.2	46.3	42.3	42.6	52.4
Thailand	28.6	31.2	36.5	21.9	39.8	39.8	37.5
Outright forward and foreign exchange swap: % of turnover							
Indonesia	45.9	13.3	56.8	37.1	33.8	31.7	47.0
Malaysia	69.7	57.4	49.2	50.2	43.3	52.7	79.2
Philippines	53.1	56.6	48.8	53.0	37.0	56.0	46.9
Thailand	68.9	68.0	55.5	75.8	57.5	58.1	61.0

Notes Spot transactions and forward and swap do not sum up to 100%. The balance includes other financial derivatives such as currency swap, options, and other products
Source BIS (various years)

Table 3 Share of foreign exchange market turnover by counterparty in selected Southeast Asian countries, in April 2016

	Local dealers	Dealers abroad	Other financial institutions	Non-financial customers
Indonesia	31.0	42.0	5.9	21.2
Malaysia	25.7	32.9	25.3	16.0
Philippines	42.0	28.8	18.3	10.9
Thailand	31.6	31.5	16.5	20.4

Source BIS (various issues)

than the underlying trade flows in these countries. The market turnover to exports ratios in 2013 were approximately nine times (Indonesia), 13 times (Malaysia), and 17 times (the Philippines and Thailand). Interdealer trading is a driving force of the forex market development in the ASEAN-4 forerunner countries.

3 Unofficial Forex Market

While all ASEAN-4 countries had unofficial forex markets, how did they differ from that of Myanmar? First, we define an unofficial forex market and classify motivations behind informal currency deals. Second, we present a generic form of unofficial forex market to contrast its functions with those of a bank-based forex market. Third, we compare the unofficial forex markets in ASEAN-4 and Myanmar, using the concept of the informal interfirm-based forex market.

3.1 Causes of Unofficial Market Formation

The unofficial forex market is where the demand for foreign exchange not accommodated in the official market meets with the unofficial supply. Various types of exchange restrictions motivate informal currency deals. We classify the underlying causes of informal currency deals into three categories: (i) exchange restrictions that regulate the official exchange rate, (ii) exchange restrictions that affect the uses and sources of foreign exchange, and (iii) licensing of foreign exchange dealers.

The first cause involves the exchange rate arrangements, in which authorities target the exchange rate to a specific level or band (Kiguel and O'Connell 1995). When the official exchange rate overvalues the domestic currency *vis-à-vis* foreign currencies, excess demand for foreign exchange arises in the official market. To preserve international reserves, authorities need to restrict access to the official market. Those who are not allocated enough foreign exchange turn to the unofficial market, where foreign exchange is traded at a premium.

A parallel premium—the gap between the official and unofficial exchange rates—encourages foreign exchange earners to sell their export proceeds in the unofficial market; the wider the gap, the more tightly authorities have to enforce the surrender requirement on exporters as well as their scrutiny of the foreign exchange allocation to importers. As foreign exchange rationing intensifies, the importance of the official exchange rate as a price signal diminishes.

The second cause involves controls to restrict the uses of foreign exchange, including prohibitions on imports of certain goods and bans on capital account transactions (Montiel et al. 1993; Agenor and Haque 1996). There are various policies in this area. Import controls range from a complete ban to controls by quotas. High tariffs and duties also encourage illegal imports for tax evasion. Another is capital controls that ban domestic residents from holding foreign assets. Because authorized dealer banks do not sell foreign exchange for illegal uses, domestic residents trying to circumvent these controls turn to the unofficial market, where they raise foreign exchange to settle payments for illegal purchases of foreign goods and assets. Likewise, banks do not accept foreign exchange revenues from exports of contraband goods and smuggling, and they are therefore traded in the unofficial market.[7]

Under the second type of policy, multiple markets with multiple exchange rates generally arise when the authorities restrict the uses and sources of foreign exchange (Canales-Kriljenko 2004). For example, when an anti-money laundering regulation prohibits banks from accepting foreign exchange revenues from illegal sources, they are traded outside banks. As such, a restriction precludes arbitrage between segments of the market, and exchange rates can differ between segments, giving rise to multiple exchange rates.

The third type of policy that shapes the unofficial forex market is foreign exchange dealer licensing. It is illegal for buyers and sellers to engage in currency deals with those who do not have a dealer license. Banks are the most common authorized dealers, who operate under regulations allowing them to sell and buy foreign exchange only for (from) legitimate uses (sources). Currency deals with unauthorized parties can be motivated by a parallel premium and illegal sources and uses of foreign exchange.

Additionally, currency deals with unauthorized parties might be preferred for other reasons, in particular, lower transaction costs. For example, when authorities issue foreign exchange dealer licenses to a small number of banks, they may seek oligopolistic rents in customer dealing by setting a wide bid–ask spread. A higher transaction cost in the official market may encourage informal currency deals outside banks.

We can summarize three dimensions of informal currency deals as in Table 4. Some informal currency deals are due to controls on exchange rates and foreign exchange rationing (the first dimension) and other deals motivated by illegal sources and uses of foreign exchange (the second dimension). These two types of currency deals should always combine the third dimension of unauthorized dealing counter-

[7] See Grosse (1992) for the foreign exchange black market that trades foreign currency receipts from illegal exports.

Table 4 Three dimensions of unofficial foreign exchange market

Dimension	Official market	Unofficial market
(1) Price of foreign exchange	Within restricted range	With premium over official rate
(2) Sources and uses of foreign exchange	Legal sources and uses	Illegal sources and uses
(3) Trading of foreign exchange	Authorized dealers	Unauthorized buyers/sellers

Source Author

parties because authorized dealers do not sell and buy foreign exchange for (from) illegal uses (sources), nor at prices outside the restricted band. By contrast, currency deals involving unauthorized counterparties (the third dimension) may not combine the other two dimensions when foreign exchange for (from) legitimate use (source) is traded at prices within the bid–ask spread of the official market.

3.2 Market Structure

By contrasting the structure of the unofficial forex market with that of the bank-based market, we clarify the peculiar features of the latter. The unofficial market has two distinctive features. First, it includes direct deals between non-financial firms, such as exporters and importers. Second, informal currency deals, by their nature, rely on a private enforcement mechanism. Currency deals are subject to the settlement risk; sellers may not deliver dollars, or buyers may fail to make payments. Due to the settlement risk, sellers would deal with only a narrower circle of counterparties, where deals are enforceable via the private enforcement mechanism.[8]

The unofficial market that is based on the private enforcement mechanism may result in market segmentation and disintegration as illustrated in Fig. 2. In this figure, there are three types of players: exporters, importers, and brokers. Exporters sell foreign exchange to importers, and the latter make payments in the local currency. This figure illustrates two types of trade. One is a direct trade between exporters and importers, depicted by an arrow with a continuous line. The other is a brokered trade, in which a broker introduces buyers to sellers, depicted by an arrow with a dotted line. This figure is deliberately drawn to produce two clusters: a cluster of Brokers X and the other of Y. There are no transactions between the two clusters, indicating market segmentation.

While both bank-based and unofficial forex markets are decentralized, the latter is more prone to segmentation. A decentralized market means that numerous

[8]The settlement risk is low in foreign currency banknote trading because spot transactions can be completed immediately. However, there remains a risk that the banknotes used in a deal are counterfeit.

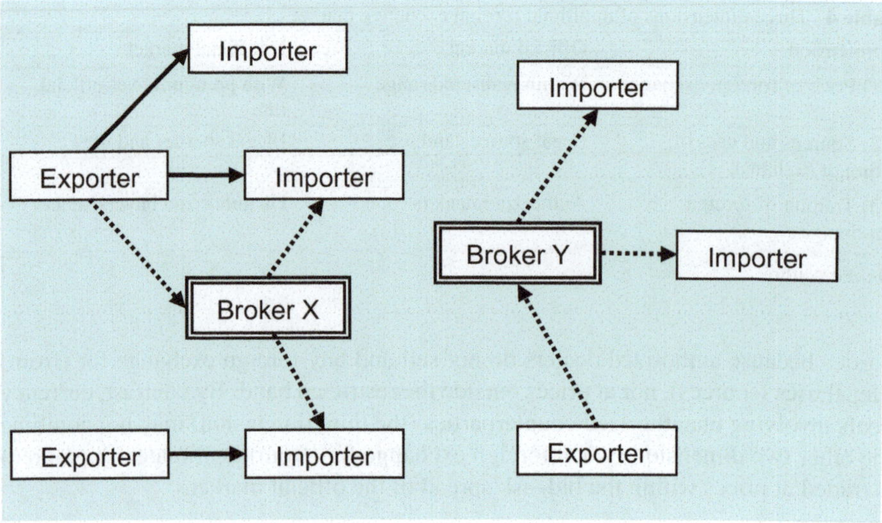

Fig. 2 A generic unofficial foreign exchange market. *Source* Author

currency deals take place concurrently at different prices. However, the bounds of dealing counterparties are narrow for the unofficial market. Informal currency deals are constrained to partners with whom the private enforcement mechanism works. This exacerbates market segmentation and inefficient foreign exchange allocation.

We introduce another dimension of the unofficial forex market, that is, the size of the unofficial market relative to the official market. In its analysis of foreign exchange policy reforms, the IMF (2003) presumes that the unofficial market consists of the margin of the official market and that is of relatively small size. However, there can be cases where the unofficial market reaches a critical mass and obtains high liquidity. For countries where the unofficial forex market is on par with the official market or overwhelms it, we call it the informal interfirm-based forex market.

The impact of foreign exchange policy reforms on the market structure would differ between the informal interfirm-based market and the bank-based market. In the latter case, informal currency deals are in the first or the second dimensions coupled with the third dimension of Table 4. The transaction costs of informal deals would be higher than those of the official market are because they need to circumvent authorities' oversight. Once the underlying causes—exchange rate controls, restrictions on imports of certain goods, or controls on capital account transactions—are lifted, informal currency deals would switch to official customer dealing. By contrast, in the informal interfirm-based forex market, informal currency deals of the 3rd dimension may remain due to their lower transaction costs compared with official customer dealing. As the informal interfirm-based forex market would acquire positive externality, informal currency deals would persist.

3.3 Unofficial Markets in the ASEAN-4 Forerunners

Informal currency deals are common in developing economies. In their seminal work, Reinhart and Rogoff (2004) document that among the countries classified as having a pegged exchange rate regime before 1997, the de facto regime was a floating exchange rate in many cases, after accounting for the unofficial market.

The unofficial forex market was also common in the ASEAN-4 forerunners as well (Diamandis et al. 2007). In the Philippines, the unofficial market was linked to corruption as a source of foreign exchange and capital flight as the underlying demand for foreign exchange. In Indonesia, although capital controls were lifted as early as the 1980s, corruption and capital flight were primary sources and uses of foreign exchange in the unofficial market. In Indonesia and Malaysia, import restrictions and import taxes stimulated demand for foreign exchange in the unofficial market. In Thailand, narcotics-related activities were a source of foreign exchange in the unofficial market.

There are two measures to infer the significance of the unofficial forex market; one is the gap between the official and unofficial market exchange rates, and the other is the size of the unofficial market (Reinhart 2002). Regarding the former, Kiguel and O'Connell (1995) argue that the significance of the unofficial market for the economy depends on the parallel premium—the gap between the official and unofficial exchange rates. As the gap expands, transactions at the official rate are more heavily controlled, while more incentives arise to sell foreign exchange in the unofficial market for the parallel premium.

With regard to the second measure, Reinhart (2002) emphasizes the need to estimate the size of the unofficial market as it may not always be in proportion to the parallel premium. In some cases, transactions in the unofficial market are limited regardless of a high parallel premium. For instance, Buehn and Eichler (2011) present empirical evidence that high financial penalties for illegal trade act as a deterrent and reduce informal currency deals irrespective of the parallel premium.

One approach to estimate the size of an unofficial forex market that Reinhart (2002) proposes is export mis-invoicing, which is the gap between a country's reported exports and its trading partners' reported imports. The revenues from unreported and under-reported exports are considered to be traded unofficially. However, there are two methodological limitations in this approach. First, because the quality of trade statistics for developing countries especially in earlier years is poor, discrepancies do not necessarily represent export mis-invoicing. Second, there are sources of foreign exchange for the unofficial market besides export mis-invoicing, including workers' remittances via informal channels and illegal capital inflows. Since there are no alternative figures available, however, we estimate the size of the unofficial market in the ASEAN-4 forerunners with the export mis-invoicing assumption.

Figure 3 depicts the gap in the official and unofficial exchange rates in the ASEAN-4 forerunner countries. The parallel premium as a percentage of the official exchange rate is occasionally high in Indonesia and the Philippines. The trends in the premium

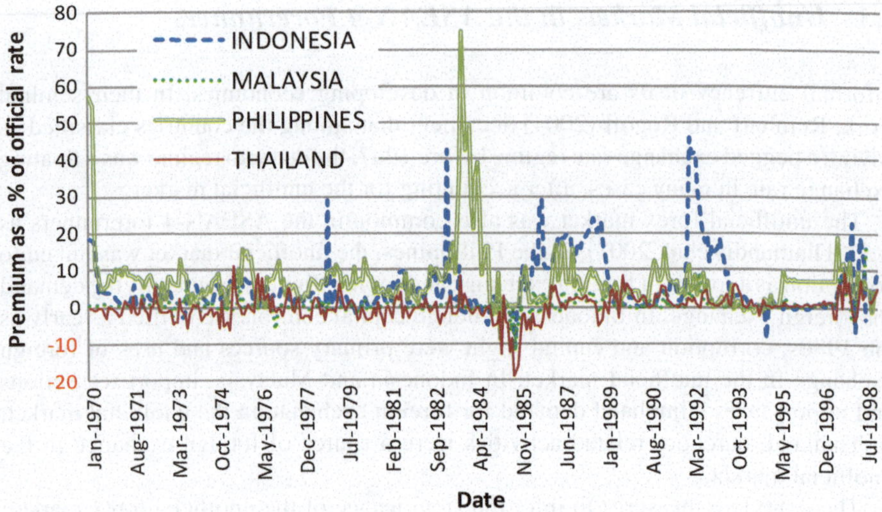

Fig. 3 Parallel market premium in selected Southeast Asian countries, 1970–1998. *Source* Reinhart (2002)

imply that these countries effectively pegged their home currencies to the U.S. dollar and adjusted the official exchange rates only occasionally. In Malaysia, the premium was relatively low, below 10%. In Thailand, the parallel premium was mostly negative, which is consistent with the inference that the proceeds from narcotics-related activities, which banks did not accept, were a major source of foreign exchange in the unofficial market. In comparison, the parallel premium in Myanmar (not depicted in the figure) in the 1990s was above 1000%.

Next, Table 5 shows some estimates of export mis-invoicing for the ASEAN-4 forerunners in 1990 and 2000, which are compiled using the United Nations Commodity Trade (UN Comtrade) database. For 1990, the reported ASEAN-4 exports mostly exceeded their trading partners' records of imports from them. These could be attributable to inaccurate reporting by trade partner countries, especially when they were developing countries. For 2000, the discrepancies are still small. These suggest that export mis-invoicing was not a significant source of foreign exchange supply to the unofficial market.

The data for the parallel premium and export mis-invoicing suggest that the unofficial forex market in the ASEAN-4 forerunners had a certain scale, especially in the Philippines, but not so much as to rival the official forex market. The prevalence of informal currency deals in Myanmar shown in subsequent chapters will make a sharp contrast with the unofficial forex market in the ASEAN-4 forerunners.

Table 5 Export mis-invoicing of selected Southeast Asian countries

Year	Exporting country	Exporter report	Partner country report	Trade mis-invoicing ratio
		Exports value (US$ million)	Imports value (US$ million)	
1990	Indonesia	25,675	17,045	166
2000	Indonesia	62,124	66,595	103
1990	Malaysia	29,453	20,493	158
2000	Malaysia	98,230	119,129	91
2000	Philippines	38,078	47,040	89
1990	Thailand	23,069	10,498	242
2000	Thailand	68,819	75,175	101

Note In the trade mis-invoicing ratio calculation, export value is multiplied by 1.1 to account for shipping costs
Source UN Comtrade (n.d.)

4 Research Question and Its Rationale

Focusing on the difference between the informal interfirm-based and bank-based forex market, this book traces the evolution of Myanmar's forex market. After presenting the research question, we state the rationale for exploring it.

4.1 *Research Question*

How does the evolution of the informal interfirm-based forex market in Myanmar differ from that of the conventional bank-based forex market? In particular, in a country where all private sector currency deals occurred in the unofficial market and banks did not offer customer dealing, how can authorities provide private firms with incentives to switch from their accustomed informal direct deals to official customer dealing at authorized dealer banks? These are the questions that this book explores in the subsequent chapters.

It is expected that in a bank-based forex market, lifting the underlying exchange restrictions eradicates informal currency deals. By devaluing the official exchange rate (the first dimension of an unofficial market) and by liberalizing imports and capital account transactions (the second dimension of an unofficial market), entities trading foreign exchange in the unofficial market would move to the official forex market. It would also accompany the unification of exchange rates.

There are at least implicit assumptions behind this prediction. First, transaction costs for currency deals would be higher in informal deals than in official customer dealing. For example, under-invoicing is costly because it is subject to penalties when detected by the authorities. The higher costs of informal currency deals would no longer pay once the underlying exchange restrictions are lifted. Second, the unofficial market would be only for a fraction of current and capital international transactions. The bulk of transactions would take place at banks. Accordingly, the official market has higher liquidity compared to the unofficial market, which would maintain the former's competitiveness.

However, these assumptions do not hold in the countries with informal interfirm-based forex markets, including Myanmar. The official banking sector is in the nascent stage of development, and the bulk of currency deals take place outside banks (the third dimension of an unofficial market), so transaction costs would not always be lower in the official market than in the unofficial market. In this context, easing exchange restrictions would not necessarily eradicate informal currency deals.

4.2 *Rationale for Research Question*

Before proceeding to the analysis, it is worth questioning the rationale for formalizing the informal forex market: is the transition from the informal interfirm-based to the official bank-based forex market necessary for Myanmar? To address this question, we list some benefits and costs of the informal interfirm-based forex market.

Regarding benefits, the sizable unofficial market in Myanmar has liquidity and has acquired positive externality which reduces transaction costs such as the cost to search for a trading counterparty. The more currency deals take place in the unofficial market, the more easily buyers and sellers can find counterparties. Besides, informal direct deals save the bank margin.

However, there are some potential costs of the unofficial market. The bounds of currency deals can be narrow; buyers and sellers trade foreign exchange only with the counterparties with whom the private enforcement mechanism works. This could exacerbate market segmentation and inefficient foreign exchange allocation.

Furthermore, a market relying on the private enforcement mechanism is not compatible with more sophisticated trades in financial derivatives such as forward and swap contracts. When the market remains in spot transactions, participants are exposed to the exchange rate risk. As Sect. 2 shows, in the modern bank-based forex market in emerging countries such as the ASEAN-4 forerunners, most currency deals are forward and swap contracts. Financial derivative trading requires sound settlement arrangements which are not compatible with the unofficial market. Overall, while the informal interfirm-based forex market exhibits some efficiency, the potential benefits from formalizing the forex market would justify the reforms.

Finally, the informal interfirm-based forex market is not unique to Myanmar. Among the 93 countries in Reinhart's (2002) dataset for which the data of parallel premium in the 1990s are available, six countries had a parallel premium over 1000%. Such a high parallel premium implies widespread informal currency deals and a little role of the official market. Apart from Myanmar, these countries include the Democratic Republic of Congo, the Islamic Republic of Iran, Iraq, Liberia, and

Surinam. This list of countries overlaps with those that Collier (2007) labels fragile states where the government has a weak capacity to implement regulations. The informal interfirm-based forex market might be, to some extent, a typical policy issue in these fragile states. Some lessons learned from Myanmar's experience might provide us with implications for foreign exchange policy reforms in these countries.

5 Outline of This Book

After a brief overview of the Myanmar economy, this section presents the plan of this book.

5.1 Overview of the Myanmar Economy

Myanmar (then Burma) pursued a variant of a centrally planned economy in 1974–1988. During this period, only the state sector was allowed to undertake international trade. Partially due to its inward-looking economic policy and economic mismanagement, the country was in and balance of payments and external debt crises in the 1980s, thus gaining the least developed country status (Myat Thein 2004).

In the midst of a deep economic downturn in September 1988, the military staged a coup d'état. Once assuming office, it commenced economic reforms for a transition to a market-based economy. However, the incomplete reforms stimulated large informal economic activities. While legalizing international trade in the private sector, the junta left intact the overvalued official exchange rate pegged to the IMF's special drawing right (SDR) and the central administration of foreign exchange allocation in the state sector.[9] The junta let all foreign currency trading in the private sector take its course.

Nonetheless, the junta imposed extensive exchange restrictions on the private sector to affect their uses of foreign exchange. The restrictions eventually stimulated smuggling and informal money transfers in addition to informal currency deals, which further complicated the forex market structure.

---

[9]The value of the SDR was based on a basket of major currencies. As the exchange rate of the U.S. dollar *vis-à-vis* the SDR fluctuated, the exchange rate of the Myanmar kyat—pegged to the SDR—also fluctuated against the U.S. dollar between 5 and 6 kyats per U.S. dollar. In the unofficial market, the kyat depreciated chronically from around 40 kyats per U.S. dollar in 1988 to above 1300 kyats in 2007.

5.2 Outline of This Book

We aim to shed light on the peculiar structure of Myanmar's forex market and investigate the root causes that yield persistent informal currency deals in the post—2011 reform period. Chapters 2–4 investigate how the informal interfirm-based forex market emerged and how it functioned. Chapters 5 and 6 evaluate the progress of foreign exchange policy reforms in reshaping the forex market since 2011. Based on findings in the preceding analyses, Chap. 7 offers prospects for modernizing the forex market.

Chapter 2 illustrates the origin of the informal interfirm-based forex market. Myanmar's transition from a planned economy was incomplete and inconsistent. While partially liberalizing the private sector's international trade and business, the central administration of the state sector was maintained. As a result, two resource allocation systems coexisted. Besides the central administration of foreign exchange in the state sector at the official exchange rate, all currency deals in the private sector were left outside banks at free market exchange rates. Because informal currency deals were the sole option for currency exchange in the private sector, an informal interfirm-based forex market emerged and acquired liquidity.

Chapter 3 analyzes the functions of the informal interfirm-based forex market. The junta implemented pervasive exchange restrictions to influence the private sector's uses of foreign exchange. On the one hand, the exchange restrictions segmented the unofficial forex market further into several parts; at least four categories of foreign exchange were traded for different purposes at different prices. On the other hand, the exchange restrictions stimulated informal economic activities as the private sector tried to circumvent such restrictions. Moreover, complementarity existed among informal currency deals, smuggling, and informal money transfers.

Complementing the analysis of the forex market organization, Chap. 4 sheds light on how exchange restrictions affected the trends in unofficial market exchange rates. Myanmar thrived with export booms of natural gas and jade in the 2000s, which coincided with an extraordinary appreciation of the Myanmar kyat vis-à-vis the U.S. dollar. Based on the qualitative analysis of the economic environment, it is shown that the exchange restrictions that initially intended to cope with a shortage in foreign exchange exacerbated the real exchange rate appreciation unnecessarily.

Chapter 5 presents the outline of the first-ever holistic foreign exchange policy reform since 2011, which included devaluation of the official exchange rate and licensing private banks for foreign exchange dealing. Drawing on financial statistics, the chapter illustrates the prevalence of informal currency deals outside banks and the linkage between the official and unofficial forex markets.

Chapter 6 analyzes the firms' behaviors in choosing between the official and unofficial forex markets for their currency deals. By identifying the characteristics of the firms remaining in informal currency deals, it sheds light on the persistence of the unofficial forex market.

Based on the trace of the informal interfirm-based forex market revealed in the preceding analyses, Chap. 7 offers prospects for modernizing Myanmar's forex market and discusses conditions for banks to replace the informal currency deals. It concludes by setting out the limitation of analyses in this book and the agenda for future research.

References

Agenor, P. R., & Haque, N. U. (1996). Macroeconomic management with informal financial markets. *International Journal of Finance and Economics, 1*(2), 87–101.

Ariyoshi, A., Habermeier, K., Laurens, B., Otker-Robe, I., Canales-Kriljenko, J. I., & Kirilenko, A. (2000). *Capital controls: Country experiences with their use and liberalization*. Occasional Paper 199. Washington, DC: International Monetary Fund.

Bank for International Settlements (BIS). (various issues). *Triennial Central Bank Survey of foreign exchange and derivative market activity*. Basel: Bank for International Settlements.

Buehn, A., & Eichler, S. (2011). Trade misinvoicing: The dark side of world trade. *The World Economy, 34*(8), 1263–1287.

Canales-Kriljenko, J. I. (2004). *Foreign exchange market organization in selected developing and transition economies: Evidence from a survey*. IMF working paper WP/04/4. Washington, DC: International Monetary Fund.

Collier, P. (2007). *The bottom billion*. New York: Oxford University Press.

Diamandis, P., Kouretas, G., & Zarangas, L. (2007). Dual foreign currency markets and the role of expectations: Evidence from the Pacific Basin countries. *Research in International Business and Finance, 21*(2), 238–259.

Ding, J. (1998). China's foreign exchange black market and exchange flight: Analysis of exchange rate policy. *The Developing Economies, 36*(1), 24–44.

Eichengreen, B. (2001). Capital account liberalization: What do cross-country studies tell us? *World Bank Economic Review, 15*(3), 341–365.

Fischer, S. (2001). Exchange rate regimes: Is the bipolar view correct? *Journal of Economic Perspectives, 15*(2), 3–24.

Ghosh, A. R., Gulde, A.-M., & Wolf, H. C. (2002). *Exchange rate regimes: Choices and consequences*. Cambridge, MA, and London: MIT Press.

Grosse, R. (1992). Colombia's black market in foreign exchange. *World Development, 20*(8), 1193–1207.

Henry, P. B. (2007). Capital account liberalization: Theory, evidence, and speculation. *Journal of Economic Literature, 45*(4), 887–895.

Hori, M., & Wong, Y. C. (2013). Costs of Myanmar's multiple exchange-rate regime. *Journal of International Trade and Economic Development, 22*(2), 209–233.

International Monetary Fund (IMF). (various issues). *Annual report on exchange arrangements and exchange restrictions*. Washington, DC: International Monetary Fund.

IMF. (1999). *Exchange rate arrangements and currency convertibility: Developments and issues, world economic and financial surveys*. Washington, DC: International Monetary Fund.

IMF. (2003). *Exchange arrangements and foreign exchange markets: Developments and issues, World Economic and Financial Surveys*. Washington, DC: International Monetary Fund.

Kenen, P. B. (Ed.). (1998). *Should the IMF pursue capital-account convertibility?* Essays in International Finance No. 207. Princeton, NJ: Princeton University.

Kiguel, M., & O'Connell, S. A. (1995). Parallel exchange rates in developing countries. *World Bank Research Observer, 10*(1), 21–52.

Kubo, K. (Ed.). (2017). *Dollarization and de-dollarization in transitional economies of Southeast Asia*. Cham: Palgrave Macmillan.

Luca, C. (2000). *Trading in the global currency markets*. Paramus, NJ: Prentice Hall.

Lyons, R. (2001). *The microstructure approach to exchange rates*. Cambridge, MA, and London: MIT Press.

McKinnon, R., & Schnabl, G. (2004). The East Asian dollar standard, fear of floating, and original sin. *Review of Development Economics, 8*(3), 331–360.

Mehran, H., Quintyn, M., Nordman, T., & Laurens, B. (1996). *Monetary and exchange system reforms in China: an experiment in gradualism*. IMF Occasional Paper No. 141. Washington, DC: International Monetary Fund.

Montiel, P. J., Agenor, P.-R., & Haque, N. U. (1993). *Informal financial markets in developing countries: A macroeconomic analysis*. Oxford and Cambridge, MA: Blackwell.

Myat Thein. (2004). *Economic development of Myanmar*. Singapore: Institute of Southeast Asian Studies.

Nguyen, T. P., & Nguyen, D.-T. (2009). Exchange rate policy in Vietnam 1985–2008. *ASEAN Economic Bulletin, 26*(2), 137–163.

Reinhart, C. (2002). *A modern history of exchange rate arrangements: Parallel markets and dual and multiple exchange rates*. Unpublished manuscript, University of Maryland.

Reinhart, C., & Rogoff, K. (2004). The modern history of exchange rate arrangements: A reinterpretation. *Quarterly Journal of Economics, 119*(1), 1–48.

Turnell, S. (2009). *Fiery dragons: Banks, moneylenders and microfinance in Burma*. Copenhagen: NIAS Press.

Turnell, S. (2011). Fundamentals of Myanmar's macroeconomy: A political economy perspective. *Asian Economic Policy Review, 6*(1), 136–153.

United Nations (UN Comtrade). (n.d.). UN Comtrade Database. https://comtrade.un.org/.

Williamson, J. (2000). *Exchange rate regimes for emerging markets: Reviving the intermediate option*. Washington, DC: Institute for International Economics.

Chapter 2
Piecemeal Reforms in the 1990s and Forex Market Segmentation between State and Private Sectors

Abstract Myanmar's unofficial forex market stemmed from piecemeal reforms during the initial stage of its transition from a planned to a market-based economy. While partially liberalizing international trade by the private sector, the government left intact the overvalued official exchange rate and the central administration of foreign exchange allocation in the state sector. All foreign currency deals made by the private sector took place outside the official system at unofficial exchange rates. As a result, the foreign exchange market was segmented into two parts—the private sector with unofficial market rates and the state sector with the official exchange rate. After a failed attempt to devalue the official rate using foreign exchange certificates in the 1990s, the authorities did not recognize the free market exchange rate, which spurred the unregulated development of the unofficial forex market.

Keywords Burmese way to socialism · Transition · Market segmentation
Foreign exchange certificate · Myanmar

1 Introduction

This chapter explores the origins of the unofficial forex market and the function of dual exchange rates in Myanmar. The unofficial forex market emerged in the process of the country's transition from a variant of a centrally planned to a market-based economy in the late 1980s and the early 1990s. The authorities did not devalue the official exchange rate and continued to apply it to the fiscal accounting in the state sector while tolerating the private sector trading foreign exchange at free market rates. The incomplete reform segmented the foreign exchange market between the state and private sectors. In terms of disparity between the official and unofficial exchange rates, Myanmar was one of the worst cases in the world.

This chapter draws on Kubo (2013) with the permission of the publisher, Taylor & Francis Ltd, http://www.tandfonline.com.

K. Kubo, *Myanmar's Foreign Exchange Market*,
https://doi.org/10.1007/978-981-13-1789-7_2

In Chap. 1, we point out three areas of policies that give rise to informal currency deals. One involves exchange rate targeting by the authorities, while another involves statutory controls on the uses and sources of foreign exchange.[1] Although both types of policies were present in Myanmar, this chapter focuses on the former, while Chap. 3 examines the latter.

This chapter is structured as follows. Section 2 illustrates Myanmar's piecemeal reforms in its transition from a planned to a market-based economy in the late 1980s and early 1990s. We show that the initial reforms were palliative, leading to the emergence of the unofficial forex market. Section 3 overviews the macroeconomic environment in the initial stage of economic transition and documents the widening gap between the official and unofficial exchange rates. Section 4 describes the junta's attempt at exchange rate unification in the mid-1990s. Section 5 discusses distortionary impacts, if any, of the official exchange rate on the private sector. Section 6 summarizes the analyses of the chapter.

2 The Myanmar Way to Its Transition to a Market Economy: Late 1980s and Early 1990s

To see how the unofficial forex market stemmed from the piecemeal transitional reforms, we first illustrate the economic environment before the transition and then outline the junta's transition strategies in the initial stage.

2.1 *Before Transition*

Until 1988, Myanmar (then Burma) pursued a variant of central planning called "the Burmese Way to Socialism" which oriented industrialization under the auspices of nationalization of the economy (Tin Maung Maung Than 2007). In this regime, the industrial and service sectors, as well as foreign trade, were monopolized by the state and were all controlled by the central planning office.

The country had a predominantly agrarian economy. While the state dominated the industrial and service sectors, the state accounted for merely 21.7% of the gross domestic product (GDP) in the period before the transition, which was similar to other transitional economies in Southeast Asia, namely Lao PDR and Vietnam (Rana 1995: 1159). The agricultural sector was never collectivized, although the government dictated the types of crops to be sown. There was a compulsory delivery system for principal crops, including rice—the country's staple diet—in which farmers delivered paddy to the government at the controlled price. The government monopolized the distribution and export of such crops. The compulsory delivery

[1] The third area is foreign exchange dealer licensing.

and distribution system of rice, however, accompanied an unofficial parallel market (Tin Soe and Fisher 1990).

The central planning regime over 1975–1988 was a hybrid planned economy prone to inflation. On the one hand, the shortage of foreign exchange resulted in a paucity of input materials and low capacity utilization of state economic enterprises (SEEs), which further translated into a shortage of final SEE products. On the other hand, the country's central planning authorities did not implement cash and credit plans; instead, SEEs maintained their working capital and obtained loans from the state banking system. A state bank—the Myanma Economic Bank (MEB)—channeled funds contingent on instructions from the central planning office. Owing to unviable investment projects and low capacity utilization, underperforming SEEs accumulated staggering debts that amounted to 9% of the GDP in 1978, which rose to 61% of GDP by 1988. As MEB's primary source of funding was the credit from the Central Bank, MEB's financing of SEE deficits was, in fact, monetization of fiscal deficit.[2]

The central planning office deployed controls on commodity prices only loosely and allowed intermittent increases in controlled prices in the face of inflation in the unofficial parallel market. The renewal of controlled prices did not keep pace with those of the parallel market. The gaps between the official and market prices brought windfall gains to those who had access to goods at official prices as they channeled them to the unofficial parallel market (Tun Wai 1996: 179).

However, the official exchange rate was treated differently. The official exchange rate was one of the most prominent official prices on which the fiscal accounting of exports and imports of the entire state sector was laid. The Myanmar kyat—the country's legal tender—was pegged to the special drawing right (SDR) of the International Monetary Fund (IMF) at 8.5057 kyats per SDR in May 1977. In the end, the official parity rate was never adjusted during the central planning regime; it was not until April 2012 that the official exchange rate was adjusted for the first time since May 1977.

During this regime, international trade by the private sector was prohibited. The private sector engaged in smuggling. The unofficial forex market traded the U.S. dollar at around 30 kyats per dollar as of 1987, whereas the official exchange rate significantly overvalued the Myanmar kyat at around 6.6 kyats per dollar (Myat Thein 2004).

2.2 *Initial Transition Strategies*

We review the junta's strategies in the initial transition period on (i) the structural reforms and (ii) the foreign exchange management.

---

[2]The deposits of the entire banking sector amounted to merely 11.3% of GDP as of 1988, although the MEB loans to SEEs reached 61%.

2.2.1 Structural Reforms

In the face of the deep recession in 1986–1988, the military staged a coup d'état in September 1988, ousted the ruling Burma Socialist Planning Party, and announced the abandonment of the Burmese Way to Socialism.[3] The military junta named itself the State Law and Order Restoration Council and was meant to be a transitional regime to revitalize the economy.[4] However, it eventually remained in office until March 2011, during which its peculiar transition strategy to a market-based economy was implemented.

A salient feature of Myanmar's transition strategy was that the junta postponed structural reforms of SEEs. In April 1989, in order to scrutinize the financial conditions of SEEs, the junta abolished their working capital accounts and started controlling their entire expenditures directly. Under the new regime, all financing of SEEs was provided by the Union Government from the State Fund Account (SFA). SEEs were required to obtain authorization from parent ministries for their expenditures. On the other hand, all receipts of SEEs were surrendered to the SFA. At the same time, the junta assumed the outstanding debts of SEEs from the MEB and converted them into the non-interest-bearing government equity. Since then, SEEs have been prohibited from taking loans. The partial reform in 1989 was aimed at containing the SEEs' deficit.

However, the partial reform aggravated the SEEs' soft budget constraint problem. Since their accounts were integrated into the state budget, SEEs were no longer accountable for their financial performances. This system induced individual SEEs to be heedless of their profits or losses.

Besides, the practice of price control was maintained for SEEs' key inputs, including petroleum and electricity, which kept their prices below the market prices. Furthermore, the planning office dictated SEEs' capital investments, using directed interest rates that were below the inflation rate. Prices of SEE products including petroleum and electricity—major inputs for many other SEEs—were set on a cost-plus basis. As SEEs delivered goods to each other according to the quotas allotted by the central planning office, controlled prices including the official exchange rate and the directed interest rates functioned as cross-subsidies among SEEs, which hid the true economic performances of individual SEEs (World Bank 1995).

The junta's controls on commodity prices were also relevant to the private sector, specifically the prices of electricity and petroleum. For example, the junta maintained the official distribution of gasoline to the private sector at the official price by quotas. The low official price of gasoline brought in excess demand and spurred the unofficial parallel market. The gap between the official price of gasoline and its parallel market price was about eightfold in 1995 (World Bank 1995: 60).

---

[3] As the Burma Socialist Planning Party was a disguised military regime led by the dictator Ne Win, the coup d'état was a turnover of government within the military regime.

[4] While the junta held a general election in May 1990 aiming for a smooth transfer of power, it did not recognize the election result. The junta changed its name to the State Peace and Development Council in November 1997.

While postponing genuine structural reforms of the existing systems, the junta emphasized the creation of new private firms and activities, but under tight state control. For example, the junta partially liberalized the domestic marketing of rice, whereas it maintained, albeit on a smaller scale, the state procurement and distribution system using the official procurement and sales prices. The junta also retained the state monopoly of rice exports, which were then the country's principal source of foreign exchange. Similarly, the junta permitted the entry of private firms into the industrial, commercial, and foreign trade sectors, whereas it promulgated the State Economic Enterprise Law in March 1989 to reserve twelve economic activities for state monopoly, including exports of teak wood, minerals, petroleum, and natural gas.

When foreign trade by private sector firms was legalized in December 1988, a policy challenge emerged relating to which exchange rate was to be applied to them. Before trade liberalization, the private sector engaged only in smuggling. The U.S. dollar was traded unofficially at around 42 kyats per dollar as of 1988, whereas the official exchange rate remained at 6.6 kyats per dollar (Myat Thein 2004). However, the junta did not address this issue.

As a consequence of the inconsistent reforms, two resource allocation systems coexisted in the country: the central planning of the state sector at the controlled prices, and the market-oriented economy of the private sector operating with free market prices. Sizable unofficial parallel markets characterized the latter.

Finally, in addition to legalizing the private sector's international trade, the junta aimed at promoting foreign investment inflows, which was in stark contrast with the previous regime's inclination toward nationalization. The junta promulgated the Foreign Investment Law as early as November 1988, which, at least ostensibly, allowed foreign investors to establish wholly owned enterprises in Myanmar. Foreign investment inflows averaged USD 175 million in 1990–1993. Foreign investments were concentrated in the oil and gas, mining, and hotel and tourism sectors.

2.2.2 Foreign Exchange Management

With regard to the foreign exchange management, the administration in the state sector remained centralized, as it had been in the planned economy regime. Exporting SEEs were forced to surrender their entire foreign currency receipts to the state budget. For any imports, SEEs were required to submit applications for Foreign Exchange permits (FE permits) to the Ministry of Finance, which scrutinized expenditures. Principal import items included petroleum and intermediate industrial goods.

Foreign exchange for the state sector was consolidated at the Myanma Foreign Trade Bank (MFTB). Any foreign currency receipts of SEEs were surrendered to the SFA within the MFTB. The exporting SEEs, in turn, were credited in Myanmar kyats for fiscal accounting, applying the official exchange rate. Similarly, importing SEEs had to present FE permits to the MFTB, which credited foreign currency from the SFA to effect international payments. In turn, they were debited in Myanmar kyats for fiscal accounting, applying the official exchange rate.

The Myanmar kyat was not convertible even within the state sector. The Ministry of Finance determined the allocation of the foreign exchange budget in the state sector by means of the FE permits. Without FE permits, SEEs could not access the foreign exchange. The official exchange rate was just a nominal figure for fiscal accounting. Even exporting SEEs had to obtain FE permits for any foreign currency expenditure, as they were not allowed to maintain revolving funds. The official exchange rate did not function to equilibrate the demand for and supply of foreign exchange.

With a view of stimulating SEEs' exports, the junta temporarily established a revolving foreign exchange fund under eight ministries in 1993, which would provide seed money for SEEs to procure imported inputs. For example, for the Myanma Timber Enterprise—one of the top foreign exchange earners among SEEs in the early 1990s—the shortage of logging facilities was a constraint to expanding exports. In such a case, the revolving fund was expected to help flexible procurements of imported inputs and boost exports. In addition, SEEs were permitted to retain additional export revenues from the revolving fund as extra-budget funds. The revolving fund amounted to nearly USD 60 million. However, SEEs still had to surrender the export revenues from other sources to the SFA at the official exchange rate. Furthermore, the revolving foreign exchange fund was abolished when the shortage of foreign exchange became exacerbated in the late 1990s.

During its transition, the junta did not devalue the official parity rate, which stood in contrast with other Asian transitional economies such as China and Vietnam.[5] The pegging of the official exchange rate to the SDR was not adjusted, and the official exchange rate remained at around 6 kyats per U.S. dollar.

Another notable feature of Myanmar's foreign exchange system in this period was that foreign exchange receipts did not routinely accumulate in the Central Bank as international reserves. The Central Bank was almost excluded from the circulation of foreign exchange in the country. Foreign exchange of the state sector had been maintained as foreign currency deposits (FCDs) of the Union Government in the SFA at the MFTB. We can state that the MFTB played the role of a foreign exchange treasury. Later, during the foreign exchange policy reforms from March 2011, the exclusion of the Central Bank from foreign exchange circulation was recognized as one of the subjects of the structural reform (IMF 2012).

Concerning the private sector, exporters were initially required to surrender 40% of their foreign currency receipts at the official exchange rate. Thus, private exporters were allowed to retain only 60% of their export earnings, which they could utilize for their own imports or sales in the unofficial market. As early as March 1990, the junta abolished the surrender requirement of private exporters (Myat Thein 2004: 155). Since then, in principle, there have been no surrender requirements on private exporters. Likewise, no foreign exchange was allocated to private importers at any time.

[5]Regarding foreign exchange policy reforms and exchange rate unification in China and Vietnam, see Mehran et al. (1996) and Dodsworth et al. (1996), respectively.

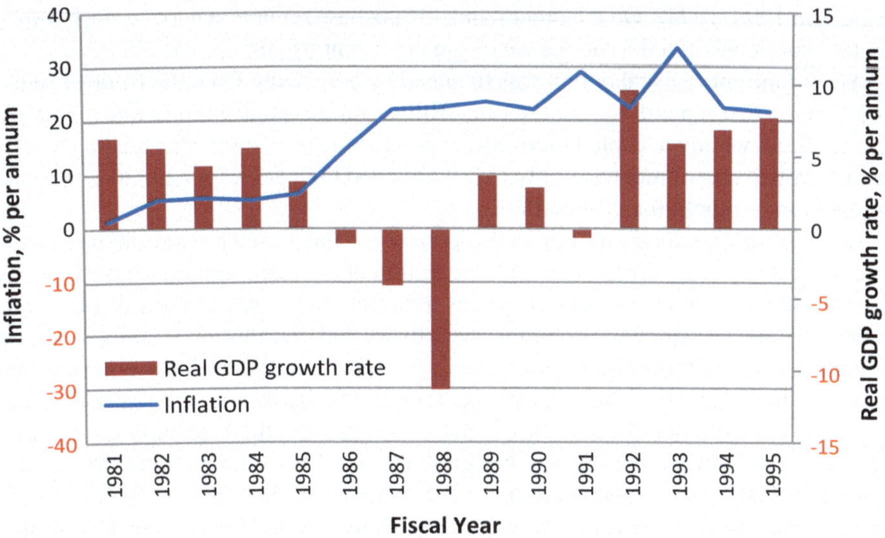

Fig. 1 Real GDP growth rate and inflation, FY 1981–1995. *Sources* World Bank (1995), Tun Wai (1996), Myat Thein (2004)

The state banks,[6] which monopolized the country's international banking, offered services including current international payments and transfers, but they did not engage in customer dealing with the private sector. Private exporters received international payments at their accounts in the state banks and maintained FCDs, and private importers ordered international payments by submitting FCDs to the state banks. This was possible as the authorities tolerated such FCD deals between private exporters and importers, which we discuss further in Chap. 3.

3 Macroeconomic Outcome of Transition in Its Initial Stage

The piecemeal reforms did not restore macroeconomic stability. Figure 1 shows the trends of the real GDP growth rate and the annual inflation rate for the period before and after the start of the transition in 1989. High inflation persisted, with an average annual inflation rate of 26.1% in 1989–1993.

Regarding the internal balance, the junta contained the fiscal deficit from an average of 8.3% of GDP in 1982–1986 to 5.8% in 1990–1994. This was mostly owing to cuts in capital expenditures by the state sector. The average capital expenditures of the state sector as a percentage of GDP declined sharply from 12.8% in 1982–1986

[6]Besides the MFTB, the Myanma Investment and Commercial Bank (MICB) was established in 1990 as a state bank whose main scope of operations included international banking services for the private sector.

to 4.0% in 1990–1994.[7] On the other hand, the tax base remained narrow, and limited tax revenues constituted a root cause of the persistent fiscal deficits.

Almost the entire fiscal deficit was financed by borrowing from the Central Bank. The Union Government issued Treasury Bills with directed interest rates, and the Central Bank wholly accepted them and expanded the base money accordingly. The annual growth rate of money supply (M2) remained high at around 25–30%, and the excess money supply fueled inflation.

Another factor behind inflation in this period was the partial relaxation of controls on commodity prices. With the notable exception of rice, agricultural marketing was liberalized, which led to rises in the prices of agricultural commodities. With regard to rice, the junta retained the compulsory delivery and distribution system, albeit on a smaller scale than during the pre-reform period. It continued monopolizing rice exports, which depressed the domestic price of rice far below the international price.

As the junta did not devalue the official exchange rate, the high inflation led to a widening gap between the official and unofficial market exchange rates. While the official exchange rate remained at around 6 kyats per U.S. dollar, in the unofficial forex market the kyat continued to depreciate from around 50 kyats per U.S. dollar in 1989 to 120 kyats in 1993. The gap between the exchange rates rose to nearly 20-fold by then.

Concerning the external balance, while the legalization of international trade by the private sector contributed to the growth of exports, it was overwhelmed by the growth of imports.[8] Trade deficits widened from an average of USD 238 million in 1986–1988 to USD 341 million in 1989–1991. Table 1 illustrates the trend of the current account. As of 1990, the private sector accounted for 42% of exports and 45% of imports of the country. On the other hand, because of the coup d'état and the illegitimacy of the junta, foreign aid was suspended from 1990 onward. The current account deficit resulted in accumulating arrears. The total stock of arrears increased from USD 0.6 billion at the end of fiscal year[9] 1991 to USD 1.5 billion by the end of the fiscal year 1994.

Exports were mostly in primary commodities such as rice, teak wood, and beans and pulses. The share of such primary commodities in total exports remained as high as 90% in the early 1990s. Diversification of exports was held back, to some extent, by restrictive controls on foreign exchange. In the face of a chronic shortage in foreign exchange, access to imported inputs was restrained, which could have

---

[7]This contraction of capital expenditures was partly due to the valuation of the expenditures in foreign currency, as they were converted into kyats at the official exchange rate while inflation continued.

[8]One of the trade promotion policies was the "import first" scheme. This scheme included the following steps. First, private importers were permitted to import goods on suppliers' credits. After selling the imported goods in the domestic market and raising the kyat revenues, the importers procured domestic goods for exports. Finally, they obtained export revenues from which they made repayments to the suppliers' credits. By 1997, this scheme was abolished and replaced with the so-called "export-first" policy.

[9]Myanmar's fiscal year runs from 1st April to 31st March.

Table 1 Current account balance, FY 1986–1994 (USD million)

	1986	1987	1988	1989	1990	1991	1992	1993	1994
Trade balance	−220	−269	−224	−119	−492	−412	−420	−606	−737
Exports	305	255	320	424	477	431	591	696	810
Of which: private sector (%)					*42*	*51*	*57*	*62*	*60*
Of which: government sector (%)					*58*	*49*	*43*	*38*	*40*
Imports	525	524	545	543	970	842	1,010	1,302	1,547
Of which: private sector (%)					*45*	*54*	*54*	*60*	*50*
Of which: government sector (%)					*55*	*46*	*56*	*40*	*50*
Service balance				−13	−110	−15	22	41	86
Receipts				141	190	180	274	247	315
Payments				154	301	195	252	206	229
Private transfers (net)				54	77	83	122	273	312
Current account balance	−204	−242	−262	−78	−526	−344	−275	−292	−339

Note The cooperative sector is included in the government sector
Sources IMF (1995), World Bank (1995), Tun Wai (1996)

deterred potential exporters in the manufacturing sector for which imported intermediate goods were indispensable.

4 Foreign Exchange Certificates and Aborted Exchange Rate Reform in the Mid-1990s

In this section, we illustrate the junta's foreign exchange policy reform comprising foreign exchange certificates (FECs) as a means to officially recognize the unofficial market rates and to effectively devalue the official rate in the mid-1990s. Caught in a dilemma between the ostensible pegging of the official exchange rate and the promotion of foreign investment, the junta introduced FECs in February 1993. According to the Foreign Exchange Regulation Act of August 1947, domestic residents were prohibited from holding foreign currency notes. At the same time, currency conversion at the overvalued official exchange rate was unrealistic for foreign investors and tourists visiting Myanmar. FECs were a temporary expedient for this dilemma. Non-resident foreigners were permitted to convert foreign currencies to FECs and make payments to domestic residents in FECs. One FEC was equivalent to USD 1.

The scope of the users of FECs was expanded from non-resident foreigners to include domestic residents. Initially, only non-resident foreigners could purchase FECs. Rather, it was compulsory for foreign travelers with tourist visas to convert a minimum of USD 300 to FECs upon arrival at the Yangon Airport.[10] In April 1993, FECs were authorized as a means for domestic residents to deposit in state banks the foreign currency receipts from unofficial sources. Prior to this, only foreign currency obtained from formal sources was permitted; foreign exchange receipts from smuggling were not accepted by banks. The regulation was amended such that foreign currency from any source could be converted to FECs (World Bank 1995: 30). Subsequently, the converted FECs, after a 10% service charge was levied, could be deposited as FCDs and used for international payments of official imports. However, the 10% service charge detracted from the convenience of FECs.

In December 1995, the junta established the official FEC exchange counter in Thein Phyu Road in Yangon, where authorized money changers were allowed to trade FECs with the kyat at free market prices. This was a de facto devaluation of the kyat. FECs were traded at prices close to the unofficial market rate of the U.S. dollar. Although the junta maintained the official exchange rate pegged to the SDR, leaving it around 6 kyats per dollar, it recognized the free market price of FECs. Thus, the junta made the kyat an officially convertible currency via FECs. The amount of FECs in circulation was equivalent to USD 2.5 million in March 1995—equivalent

[10]The amount of compulsory exchange was later reduced to USD 200 and was abolished in August 2003 (Hori and Wong 2008).

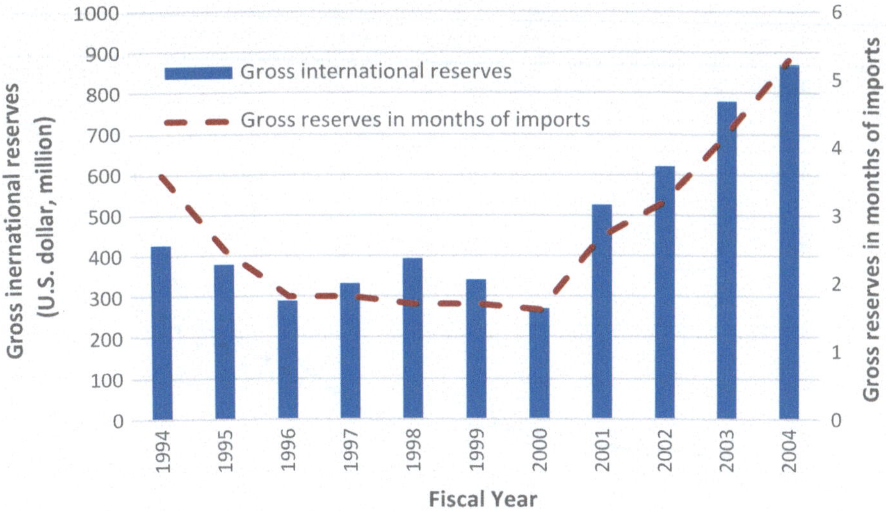

Fig. 2 International reserves, FY 1994–2004. *Sources* IMF Country Report (various issues)

to 0.035 months' worth of imports of the private sector—and it increased to USD 9.1 million in March 1997.[11]

When the Asian Financial Crisis erupted in neighboring Thailand, however, the reform momentum withered away. Even before the Asian Financial Crisis, the external balance was in deficit. Figure 2 illustrates the trend of gross international reserves in terms of the U.S. dollar and months of imports. Gross international reserves in terms of months of imports were already as low as 1.7 months at the end of the fiscal year 1996 (March 1997). These circumstances led the junta to intensify administrative controls on foreign exchange and trade. The junta used moral suasion to stabilize the exchange rate on the FEC exchange counter. Furthermore, the junta introduced caps on private imports using FECs. In July 1997, the ceiling restricted imports using FECs to USD 50,000 per month per foreign currency account, and the cap was tightened progressively to USD 30,000 in January 1999 and to USD 10,000 in August 2000 (IMF 1999; Kudo and Mieno 2009: 108).[12] Later, imports with FECs became virtually impossible; because of controls on their use, the price of FECs diverged from the unofficial market price of U.S. dollar notes.

By the end of 2001, facing a sharp depreciation of the kyat on the unofficial market, the junta ordered the authorized money changers on the FEC exchange counter to

[11]The number of FECs issued reached USD 52 million in March 1995 and USD 409.6 million in March 1997. More than 99% of FECs issued were held at banks as of March 1997 (Policy Research Institute 1999).

[12]In Myanmar, many business owners registered multiple companies in the same line of business. For example, a business owner might possess two or three export companies that exported the same varieties of commodities. Such a practice might have been related to the cap on uses of FECs per bank account.

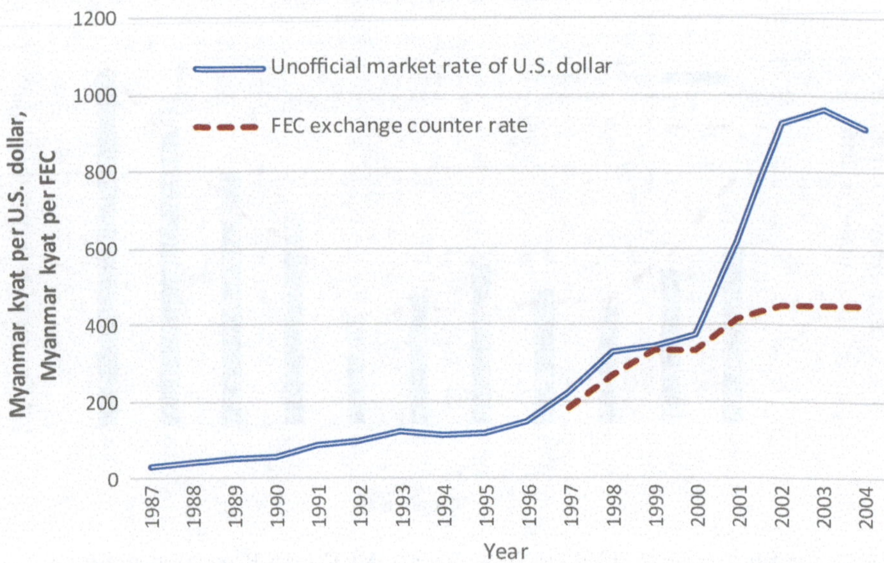

Fig. 3 Unofficial market exchange rate and FEC exchange counter rate, 1987–2004. *Note* Annual average FEC exchange counter rates for 1995 and 1996 are not available to the author. *Sources* Myat Thein (2004), Mieno (2009)

fix the price of FECs at 450 kyats, which overvalued the kyat. Figure 3 shows the trends of the prevailing unofficial market rate of U.S. dollar notes and the price of FECs on the exchange counter. The gap between the two exchange rates was more than twofold in 2002. Trading of FECs in the official exchange counter dried up and shifted to the unofficial market, which signified the end of the junta's recognition of the unofficial market exchange rate.

While FECs lost impetus as a means of official devaluation and current account convertibility, they remained legal tender for domestic transactions. Typical uses of FECs included quota-free sales of petroleum and payments of utility bills. Trading of FECs continued in the unofficial market.[13]

When the foreign exchange position of the state sector improved owing to the surge in natural gas exports in 2003 (as will be shown in Chap. 4), however, the junta did not resume the exchange rate policy reform. Certainly, some controls on foreign exchange and trade were removed, including the abolition of compulsory exchange of USD 200 to FECs for foreign visitors.[14] There was no remarkable change until the new government taking over office from the junta reopened the foreign exchange counter on Thein Phyu Road in Yangon in November 2011.

[13]In March 2013, the Central Bank announced the abolition of FECs.

[14]Other controls removed included the abolition of conditionality for imports of non-priority and priority items in the mid-2000s, which is discussed in Chap. 3.

5 Link between State and Private Sectors

Despite the glaring gap between the official and unofficial exchange rates, the private sector was mostly sheltered from its distortionary impacts; but the impact of the official exchange rate on the private sector was not nil. The ostensible fixed exchange rate regime nurtured the unofficial forex market.

5.1 Flows of Foreign Exchange from the Private to State Sector

As soon as the retention rate of private firms' export earnings was raised to 100% in April 1990, foreign currency deals in the private sector took place entirely at the unofficial market exchange rate, which insulated private firms from the foreign exchange administration system of the state sector. This sheltered the private sector from the distortionary impacts of the gap between the official and unofficial exchange rates.

Instead, the junta controlled both exports and imports of the private sector at its discretion. Private firms were required to obtain export and import licenses from the Myanmar Ministry of Commerce for every shipment. With regard to export licensing, several commodities—notably rice, teak wood, and minerals—were reserved for SEE exports. For example, rice exports from the private sector were banned until April 2003. With regard to import licensing, the junta classified imports into priority and non-priority goods and imposed conditions on imports of non-priority goods such as luxury consumer goods. Thus, the junta influenced the composition of private imports.[15]

There were several explicit channels through which the junta siphoned off foreign exchange from the private sector. In December 1994, the junta amended the commercial tax and introduced a 5% export tax payable in foreign currency. By January 1999, the export tax was raised to 10% (IMF 1999: 7).[16]

Apart from the export tax, the junta occasionally introduced surrender requirements whereby foreign exchange earners had to convert their foreign currency receipts at a discretionarily directed exchange rate. One example was the surrender requirement for foreign currency receipts from service exports, labor income, and migrant workers' remittances, which was initially 25%. In late 1994, the surrender requirement was replaced with a 10% tax (IMF 1995: 22).[17] Another was tempo-

[15] We will discuss the details of such controls in Chap. 3.

[16] To be precise, an extra 2% income tax was added to the 5% commercial tax in December 1997; the commercial tax was raised to 8% in January 1998, leading to an effective 10% export tax.

[17] This was applicable to migrant workers recruited by Myanmar government agencies. As is discussed in Chap. 3, other migrant workers used informal money transfer channels to avoid the tax.

rary surrender requirements imposed on exporters of certain commodities including fishery and garment products in the early 2000s.[18]

5.2 *Impact on the Private Sector*

While the private sector was largely sheltered from distortionary effects of the gap between the overvalued official exchange rate and the unofficial market exchange rate, there were indirect impacts of the ostensible fixed exchange rate regime on the private sector. One was the uncertainty in tax liabilities. Customs duties tended to get lower when the junta used the overvalued official exchange rate for the valuation of imported goods. As of 1996, when the unofficial market exchange rate was around 150 kyats per U.S. dollar, the official exchange rate was about 6 kyats per U.S. dollar. If the official exchange rate was applied to the valuation of goods of which the import tariff was 60%, the effective import tariff was 2.4%. In June 1996, the Myanmar Customs replaced the official exchange rate with an administrative rate of 100 kyats per dollar for the valuation of import duties.[19] In June 2004, the Myanmar Customs applied the FEC exchange center rate—450 kyats per dollar—as the valuation rate, but it had already overvalued the kyat (see Fig. 3). Subsequently, various discretionary exchange rates were applied to different categories of imported goods.

A more fundamental impact of the ostensible pegging of the kyat exchange rate was the rise of informal economic activities. By tolerating informal currency deals, the junta recognized the free market exchange rates only unofficially. This made unclear the boundary between legal and illegal economic activities in Myanmar (World Bank 1995: 19). The unofficial forex market developed in an unregulated environment. All the currency deals of the private sector were driven to the unofficial market, which augmented its liquidity.

6 Concluding Remarks

The junta's piecemeal reforms in the initial stage of transition from a planned to a market-based economy created the fundamental segmentation in the forex market between the state and private sectors. The overvalued official exchange rate was never devalued during the transition. The central administration of foreign exchange in the state sector remained, whereby the official exchange rate was applied to the fiscal accounting of international transactions. By contrast, since the abolition of

[18]In August 2000, a surrender requirement was set temporarily on 40% of export revenues of prawn exporters at the overvalued FEC exchange counter rate. Similarly, in August 2001, garment exporters were required to convert a part of export revenues at the overvalued FEC exchange counter rate for the amount equivalent to the labor costs of their factories.

[19]Ministry of Finance and Revenue Notification No. 97/96.

the surrender requirement on export receipts in March 1990, the private sector was sheltered from the overvalued official exchange rate. In principle, foreign currency deals of the private sector took place in the unofficial market.

Introducing FECs in February 1993 and officially admitting its trading at a free market price in December 1995, the junta at one point recognized the unofficial market exchange rates, which was a de facto devaluation. However, faced with a sustained depreciation of the kyat against FECs, the junta ordered authorized dealers to fix the price of FECs in 2001. Since then, the foreign exchange policy reform using FECs lost momentum.

As far as foreign currency deals in the private sector took place at unofficial market exchange rates, the private sector was sheltered from the direct impact of the gap between the official and unofficial exchange rates. Nonetheless, the impact of the ostensible pegging regime on the private sector was not nil.

One fundamental impact on the private sector came from the unclear line between legal and illegal economic activities. While the junta did not devalue the official exchange rate, it tolerated currency trading between private exporters and importers at the free market rates. The unofficial forex market was left unregulated and took its own course of development, obtaining high liquidity.

References

Dodsworth, J., Spitaller, E., Braulk, M., Lee, K., Miranda, K. M., Mulder, C. B., Shishido, H., & Srinivasan, K. (1996). *Vietnam: Transition to a market economy*. IMF occasional paper 135. Washington, DC: International Monetary Fund.

Hori, M., & Wong, Y. C. (2008). *Efficiency cost of Myanmar's multiple exchange rate regime*. IMF working paper 08/199. Washington, DC: International Monetary Fund.

IMF (International Monetary Fund). (1995). *Myanmar: Recent economic developments*. IMF country report No. 95/126. Washington, DC: International Monetary Fund.

IMF. (1999). *Myanmar: Recent economic development*. IMF country report No. 99/134. Washington, DC: International Monetary Fund.

IMF. (2012). *Myanmar: Staff report for the 2011 Article IV consultation*. IMF country report 12/104. Washington, DC: International Monetary Fund.

Kubo, K. (2013). Myanmar's two decades of partial transition to a market economy: A negative legacy for the new government. *Post-Communist Economies, 25*(3), 357–370.

Kudo, T., & Mieno, F. (2009). Trade, foreign investment and Myanmar's economic development in the transition to an open economy. In K. Fujita, F. Mieno, & I. Okamoto (Eds.), *The economic transition in Myanmar after 1988: Market economy versus state control* (pp. 103–127). Singapore: NUS Press.

Mehran, H., Guintyn, M., Nordman, T., & Laurens, B. (1996). *Monetary and exchange system reforms in China: An experiment in gradualism*. IMF occasional paper No. 141. Washington, DC: International Monetary Fund.

Mieno, F. (2009). Characteristics of capital accumulation in Myanmar, 1988–2003. In K. Fujita, F. Mieno, & I. Okamoto (Eds.), *The economic transition in Myanmar after 1988: Market economy versus state control* (pp. 23–65). Singapore: NUS Press.

Myat Thein. (2004). *Economic development of Myanmar*. Singapore: Institute of Southeast Asian Studies.

Policy Research Institute. (1999). *Current status and prospect for development of Myanmar economy*. Tokyo: Ministry of Finance of Japan (in Japanese).

Rana, P. B. (1995). Reform strategies in transitional economies: Lessons from Asia. *World Development, 23*(7), 1157–1169.

Tin Soe & Fisher, B. S. (1990). An economic analysis of Burmese rice price policies. In Mya Than & J. L. H. Tan (Eds.), *Myanmar dilemmas and options* (pp. 117–166). Singapore: Institute of Southeast Asian Studies.

Tin Maung Maung Than. (2007). *State dominance in Myanmar: The political economy of industrialization*. Singapore: Institute of Southeast Asian Studies.

Tun Wai. (1996). Part two: Myanmar. In P. B. Rana & H. Naved (Eds.), *From centrally planned to market economies: The Asian approach* (Vol. 3 Lao PDR, Myanmar and Viet Nam, pp. 149–331). Hong Kong: Oxford University Press.

World Bank. (1995). *Myanmar: Policy for sustaining economic reform*. Report No. 14062-BA. Washington, DC: World Bank.

Chapter 3
Unofficial Forex Market and Informal Economic Activities under Exchange Restrictions on the Private Sector

Abstract Exhaustive exchange restrictions affected the private sector in two ways. First, they segmented the forex market further into several parts, which led to multiple exchange rates within the unofficial market. Second, the stringent restrictions with weak enforcement eventually stimulated informal economic activities, including trade settlement diversion and smuggling, both of which were underpinned by the informal money transfer system. Our qualitative analysis unveils the diversity in informal currency deals. Some were motivated by official uses, and their prevalence added to the liquidity of the unofficial market. Others were motivated by informal economic activities including smuggling and the remittances of irregular status migrant workers; informal currency deals would persist along with the underlying informal economic activities.

Keywords Multiple exchange rates · Trade settlement diversion · Informal money transfer · U.S. economic sanctions · Myanmar

1 Introduction

In Chap. 2, we illustrate that under the ostensible fixed exchange rate regime, foreign currency deals in the private sector were left to take their course at free market exchange rates. Banks did not trade foreign exchange with the private sector, which nourished the unofficial forex market.

The unofficial forex market comprised diverse currency deals which were motivated by various economic activities, both official and unofficial. This chapter aims to provide an overview of diverse informal currency deals and discuss the sources of their persistence.

We illustrate how administrative controls on international trade and foreign exchange shaped the unofficial forex market. In stark contrast to its blind eyes to informal currency deals, the junta imposed exhaustive exchange restrictions on the private sector to cope with the chronic shortage of foreign exchange in the country.

K. Kubo, *Myanmar's Foreign Exchange Market*,
https://doi.org/10.1007/978-981-13-1789-7_3

In this chapter, we describe the administrative controls in the 1990s and 2000s and analyze how the private sector adapted to them.

We unveil two profound effects of the administrative controls on the private sector. On the one hand, they further segmented the unofficial forex market into several parts, which led to multiple exchange rates and distorted resource allocation. On the other hand, as the private sector struggled to circumvent them, the controls eventually stimulated informal economic activities including trade settlement diversion and smuggling. The informal money transfer system—*hundi*—underpinned such informal economic activities.

The remainder of this chapter is structured as follows. Section 2 reviews the administrative controls on the private sector's current international transactions. Section 3 illustrates that exchange restrictions segmented the unofficial forex market. The next two sections show how exchange restrictions stimulated informal economic activities. First, Sect. 4 shows that private exporters and importers devised trade settlement diversion to circumvent the restrictions on trade settlements, and the U.S. economic sanctions of July 2008 reinforced that practice. Section 5 analyzes the extent to which exchange restrictions gave rise to trade misreporting and smuggling. Section 6 explains the informal money transfer system that underpinned informal economic activities. Based on the preceding analyses, Sect. 7 points out the features of Myanmar's unofficial forex market that could be associated with its persistence. Section 8 summarizes the analyses and concludes the chapter.

2 Administrative Controls on the Private Sector

Exhaustive exchange restrictions on the private sector by three bodies of authorities—the Central Bank of Myanmar (CBM), the Ministry of Commerce, and the Customs Department of the Ministry of Finance and Revenue—overlapped, synthetically obstructing the private sector's international trade and stimulating their informal economic activities. This section reviews these administrative controls and illustrates exemptions in the restrictions for cross-border trade.

2.1 Administrative Controls

Three bodies of authorities administered the controls on international trade and foreign exchange in the private sector. We summarize the controls by administrative body.

2.1.1 Central Bank of Myanmar

Administrative controls by the CBM were concerned with financial and settlement instruments as well as licensing of international banking. The outdated regulations that the CBM maintained imposed severe obstacles to the private sector international trade.

First, the Foreign Exchange Regulation Act of 1947 prohibited domestic residents from holding foreign currency notes. The Act was in effect until the Foreign Exchange Management Regulation superseded it in September 2014. The Act required exporters to receive international payments via bank transfers. While exporters were permitted to retain foreign currency deposits (FCDs) at banks in the country, FCDs could not be withdrawn in foreign currency notes.[1,2] On the contrary, the banks in principle did not accept foreign currency notes for deposit either since it was illegal for domestic residents to hold them.

Second, as Chap. 2 explains, the CBM introduced foreign exchange certificates (FECs) in February 1993. FECs were legal tender. FCDs could be withdrawn in FECs. Also, the state banks accepted FECs for international payments until the Ministry of Commerce tightened import controls in July 1997 (see the next subsection).

Third, the CBM restricted foreign exchange dealer licenses to the state banks—Myanma Foreign Trade Bank (MFTB), Myanma Investment and Commercial Bank (MICB), and Myanma Economic Bank (MEB)—of which the first two were the primary vehicles for the private sector.[3] However, these banks did not buy or sell foreign exchange with the private sector given the overvalued official exchange rate; they did not convert exporters' receipts to the kyat, nor did they accept the kyat for importers' international payments.

Fourth, in relation with the Foreign Exchange Regulation Act of 1947, state banks executed importers' international payments only after their import cargo arrived in the country; the banks required importers to present the cargo arrival notice, which precluded importers' advance payments to their foreign suppliers.

---

[1] It is worth emphasizing that there were no surrender requirements on private sector exports, perhaps due to the presence of the glaringly overvalued official exchange rate.

[2] Withdrawals of FCDs in foreign currency was possible for exceptional cases such as expenditures for foreign trips.

[3] In July 1990, the Financial Institutions of Myanmar Law (The State Law and Order Restoration Council Law No. 16/90) was promulgated, and private banks were subsequently established. As of July 1995, 15 private banks were in operation, of which four were granted licenses to transact in foreign exchange (World Bank 1995: iii). However, it appears that these private banks did not engage in international banking. Furthermore, in tightening its controls on foreign exchange, the junta revoked foreign exchange dealer licenses for all private banks in March 1998 and transferred all foreign currency accounts to the MFTB or MICB (IMF 1999: 28).

2.1.2 Ministry of Commerce

Administrative controls by the Ministry of Commerce were concerned with the uses and sources of foreign exchange. Such controls were linked to the junta's intention to influence the uses of foreign exchange in the private sector.

First, both imports and exports were subject to licensing. Export/Import licenses from the Ministry of Commerce were required for every trade contract. Those who were not able to get licenses turned to smuggling. Furthermore, with regard to imports, the junta set priority goods (Schedule A), including fertilizers, cooking oil, and machinery, and non-priority goods (Schedule B), including luxury consumer goods. The junta issued import licenses for items on Schedule B on the condition that the applicant would import goods on Schedule A at least the same value as that of imports from Schedule B.[4] It was possible that the state economic enterprises procured imported inputs from the private sector using their kyat budget when the state sector was short of foreign exchange. It is believed that the regulation of priority and non-priority goods was lifted by April 2005 as the foreign exchange position of the state sector improved.[5]

Second, in July 1997, the Trade Policy Council was established with the vice chair of the junta as its head, which implemented a series of restrictions on private sector imports. The most notable restriction was the "export-first" policy that made the issuance of import licenses conditional on importers' presentation of foreign exchange whose source was official exports; that is, "export earnings." For every FCD balance, the state banks kept records of the sources of foreign exchange to distinguish "export earnings" from others. As the "export-first" policy was tightened, the Ministry did not issue import licenses to those without evidence of "export earnings" issued by the state banks.

Furthermore, the junta discretionally changed the definition of "export earnings" from time to time. For example, since January 2010, foreign currency income from services, including receipts of local hotels and tourism companies, were treated as such after a 10% income tax was paid in the foreign currency.

2.1.3 Customs Department

The Customs Department administered controls on international settlements based on the Control of Imports and Exports Act of 1947.[6] For export customs clearance, Myanmar Customs required evidence of advance payments (e.g., payment advice

[4] In March 1998, by the Ministry of Commerce Minister's Office Order No. 4/98, the import license conditionality was tightened, and the proportion of non-priority goods in Schedule B was cut to 20% of the total import permission.

[5] In the author's interviews with private importers on various occasions in 2007, the respondents stated that there was a change in the policy around this period. In Myanmar, the implementation of regulations often changed without thorough public notification.

[6] There were overlaps, though they were consistent, between this Act and the Foreign Exchange Regulation Act of 1947.

of a telegraphic transfer, or an irrevocable letter of credit (L/C)) from foreign buyers; without such evidence, export cargoes were not allowed to clear customs. This precluded foreign buyers' deferred payments to Myanmar's exporters.

The Customs Department also administered import duties and export taxes. The latter consisted of 2% of the corporate income tax[7] and 8% of commercial tax against the export value, payable in foreign currency, deducted at the state banks.[8]

2.2 *Exemption of Restrictions for Border Trade*

The Customs Department together with the Ministry of Commerce classified official trade into two categories: normal trade and border trade. Border trade refers to cross-border trade by land transport with Myanmar's four neighboring countries: Bangladesh, China, India, and Thailand.[9] Cross-border trade was illegal during the planned economy regime. It was first legalized in October 1988, when the junta signed a border trade agreement with China, followed by India and Bangladesh in 1994, and Thailand in 1996 (Kudo 2013). Normal trade refers mostly to seaborne and airborne trade.[10]

Considering the lack of international banking facilities in the remote border areas, the junta exempted two restrictions for border trade: the regulations on international trade settlements and import licensing. First, for normal trade, the international settlements had to be conducted via international bank transfers, with currencies designated by the CBM (U.S. dollar, Euro, and Singapore dollar), while this was exempted for border trade. Second, the authorities did not require "export earnings" as a condition for import licenses for border trade.

The less stringent controls on border trade more than compensated for the lack of international banking facilities in the border areas. Border trade was settled in funds from any source, usually in Chinese yuan or Thai baht in either cash or account balances at banks on the other side of the border.[11] The junta tried to establish a formal settlement channel denominated in the U.S. dollar in the border areas,[12] but

[7]This is an advance payment of the corporate income tax. The full tax liabilities are determined later based on the financial statements, and this advance payment is deductible from the total tax liabilities.

[8]Initially, the tax rate was 5%.

[9]Myanmar shares a land border with Lao PDR, but there is no customs office on the border.

[10]Technically, there can be normal trade in which shipments go through a land border, but the settlement occurs through banks using "export earnings."

[11]The U.S. dollar was seldom used for border trade settlements with China and Thailand.

[12]For example, in November 1998, in the aftermath of the Asian financial crisis, the junta issued an order requiring all border trade transactions to be conducted in U.S. dollars. In 2009, a memorandum of understanding was concluded between the Myanma Economic Bank (MEB) and Chinese state-owned banks with regard to settlements between bank branches in the border area, and the MEB opened Chinese yuan nostro accounts at branches of Chinese state-owned banks. However, border trade settlements using the MEB rarely happened.

Table 1 Trends in border trade, FY 1995–2007

	Exports (US$, mil.)			Imports (US$, mil.)		
	Total exports	Private sector	Border trade	Total imports	Private sector	Border trade
1995	895	477	43	1,832	1,236	293
1996	928	605	58	1,993	1,559	299
1997	1,036	770	155	2,309	1,645	102
1998	1,082	745	146	2,702	1,820	154
1999	1,433	1,109	196	2,605	1,833	148
2000	1,961	1,380	235	2,321	1,857	176
2001	2,549	1,333	293	2,734	1,777	213
2002	3,075	1,653	273	2,297	1,786	188
2003	2,356	1,308	300	2,235	1,532	211
2004	2,915	1,262	385	1,979	1,354	252
2005	3,554	1,603	429	1,982	1,368	282
2006	5,223	2,068	647	2,928	1,804	445
2007	6,413	2,369	747	3,347	2,443	583

Sources Central Statistical Organization (CSO) (various issues), Asian Development Bank (2001), Kudo (2013)

the efforts were mostly ineffective because a stringent control might drive official border trade underground, leading to a loss of customs duties. The different controls on border and normal trade translated into a more fundamental difference between the two types of trade with regard to the sources of funds for settlements.

Table 1 illustrates the proportions of private sector trade and border trade in the country's total exports and imports. Although not specified in the statistics, the bulk of border trade exports and imports in this period are considered to belong to the private sector. On this assumption, we estimate that border trade exports accounted for 9% of the private sector exports and 24% of the private sector imports in 1995, shifting to 31% and 24% in 2007, respectively. In addition, according to Kudo (2013), the USD 647 million of border trade exports in 2006 included USD 453 million with China, USD 158 million with Thailand, USD 11 million with India, and USD 25 million with Bangladesh.[13] Likewise, the USD 445 million of border trade imports included USD 297 million with China, USD 143 million with Thailand, USD 5 million with India, and USD 1 million with Bangladesh.

From these figures, Chinese yuan and Thai baht in the forms of cash and offshore account balances are considered to have been major commodities in the unofficial forex market.

[13]While they were recorded in terms of the U.S. dollar, it does not necessarily mean they were settled in U.S. dollar.

3 Market Segmentation within the Unofficial Market

One of the impacts of administrative controls was segmentation in the unofficial forex market further into several parts. Various categories of foreign exchange were traded for different uses at different prices.

3.1 *Classification of Foreign Currency Traded in the Unofficial Market*

The major categories of foreign currency traded in the unofficial forex market can be summarized as in Table 2. These included "export earnings," FECs, foreign currency notes, and offshore account balances. We provide some detailed accounts of "export earnings" and the others.

3.1.1 "Export Earnings"

The "export first" policy of July 1997 differentiated "export earnings" from the others. Exporters had to repatriate their receipts from official normal trade exports and to retain them as FCDs before disposal. Importers had to raise "export earning" FCDs to obtain import licenses. This environment prompted trading in "export earning" FCDs

Table 2 Categorization of foreign exchange traded in the unofficial market

Category	Possession is legal or not	Related regulations	Major sources	Major uses
Export earnings (FCDs)	Legal	• Export/import licensing	• Normal trade exports	• Normal trade imports
Foreign currency notes	Illegal	• Foreign Exchange Regulation Act of 1947	• Foreigners (U.S. dollar) • Border trade (Chinese yuan, Thai baht)	• Savings (U.S. dollar) • Border trade (Chinese yuan, Thai baht)
FECs	Legal	• Export/import licensing	• Foreigners	• Domestic payments
Offshore account balances	Illegal	• Customs' controls	• Export smuggling • Border trade export	• Import smuggling • Border trade import • Savings

Source Author

between exporters and importers. It is a unique feature of Myanmar's unofficial forex market that informally traded "export earning" FCDs were used for official imports, not for smuggling.

The authorities tolerated transfers of FCDs between domestic residents' accounts, which facilitated exporters and importers to trade "export earnings" outside banks.[14] All exporters and importers had FCD accounts at the state banks which executed account-to-account transfers for their currency deals.[15]

There were two distinctive patterns for "export earnings" trading. One was direct deals between buyers and sellers, and the other was that a broker matched buyers and sellers. Brokers served several functions in addition to matching. One was that they provided insurance against the default of a contract by the buyer/seller, taking commissions from both parties; in the event of default, they would shoulder the loss. Yet another was the diffusion of exchange rate quotes that buyers and sellers could use as a reference.

Using their original survey data of private importers, Mieno and Kubo (2016) shed light on the efficiency of the unofficial market for "export earnings." Their survey was conducted in Yangon in 2009. The population of the survey was the top 300 private importers listed as normal trade importers in the 2008 Myanmar Customs records. Of these, 100 importers were selected by snowball sampling and 95 firms provided effective answers. Among these, 78 firms (82% of the total) reported that they bought "export earnings" from exporters, whereas the remaining 17 firms sourced "export earnings" from their own exports. The figure shows the prevalence of the unofficial market. Of the 78 firms who purchased "export earnings," 66 engaged in direct deals with exporters, and 12 firms relied on brokers. Larger importers tended to engage in direct deals more often than did smaller ones. Finally, of the 78 firms, 61 firms answered that they could easily find—within a couple of hours—an alternative seller of "export earnings" other than those they had traded before. These figures imply efficiency in the unofficial forex market.

3.1.2 Other Categories

First, FECs, although initially intended for uses by foreign visitors, were traded among domestic residents in the unofficial market since the failure of the initial reform as documented in Chap. 2. Unlike "export earnings," FEC deals are considered to have been mostly between informal money changers and individuals or firms. International organizations operating in Myanmar also used FECs to pay salaries to their local employees. FECs were accepted for certain domestic payments such as

[14]There was a period when the junta restricted domestic account transfers. During that period, exporters who possessed "export earning" FCDs imported goods on behalf of importers, and importers paid exporters in the Myanmar kyat.

[15]The account transfer charge between banks, for example from MFTB to MICB, was USD 3, whereas the transfers within a bank cost USD 2.

public utility charges. However, banks did not accept FECs for international payments since the tightening of import controls.[16]

Second, U.S. dollar notes (the greenback) were traded widely in the unofficial market, and its exchange rate is considered to have functioned as the reference rate in the entire unofficial market (IMF 2012). Uses of U.S. dollar notes should include a store of value in the face of the country's chronic inflation. Deals of U.S. dollar notes were observable at informal money changers, but interfirm deals of U.S. dollar notes were not observable due to their nature.

Whether U.S. dollar notes were used for international payments is not certain for three reasons. First, under the "export-first" policy, banks did not accept U.S. dollar note for international payments. Second, for border trade, though settlements by any means were tolerated, the majority was in Chinese yuan or Thai baht cash and bank account balances. From the viewpoint of Myanmar's trading partners in China and Thailand, it is more convenient to settle trade in their local currencies. Third, it is costly to take U.S. dollar notes out of Myanmar and deposit them in offshore accounts that could be used for international payments of unofficial trade. Furthermore, under anti-money laundering regulations, foreign banks would not accept large amounts of currency notes. These factors imply that, unlike Chinese yuan and Thai baht notes, the use of U.S. dollar notes for international payments would have been uncommon.

Third, offshore account balances (cross-border deposits) can be used for international settlements of smuggling and border trade. We discuss offshore account balances in connection with informal trade settlements in Sect. 4 of this chapter.

3.2 Gaps among Unofficial Exchange Rates

Various categories of foreign currency were traded at different exchange rates in the unofficial market. Figure 1 illustrates the daily exchange rates of U.S. dollar notes, FECs, and "export earnings" for the period from August 15, 2007, to March 29, 2012. The price of FECs is that of the unofficial forex market, while its price at the official exchange counter was fixed at 450 kyats in this period. The gaps between the various unofficial market rates—multiple exchange rates—clearly demonstrate market segmentation within the unofficial market.

"Export earnings" dollars were traded at a premium above the price of the U.S. dollar notes. The premium on "export earnings" surpassed 13% in January 2010. There are two possible reasons for the premium on "export earnings." One is that "export earnings" were the only foreign currency that the state banks accepted to effect international payments. Another is that the 10% export tax, which exporters could evade if they went on smuggling, might be partially shifted to buyers.

At the same time, "export earnings" were illiquid assets that had demand only from private importers engaged in normal trade because banks effected international

[16]To be precise, FECs could be used for international payments up to certain limits. See Sect. 4 in Chap. 2.

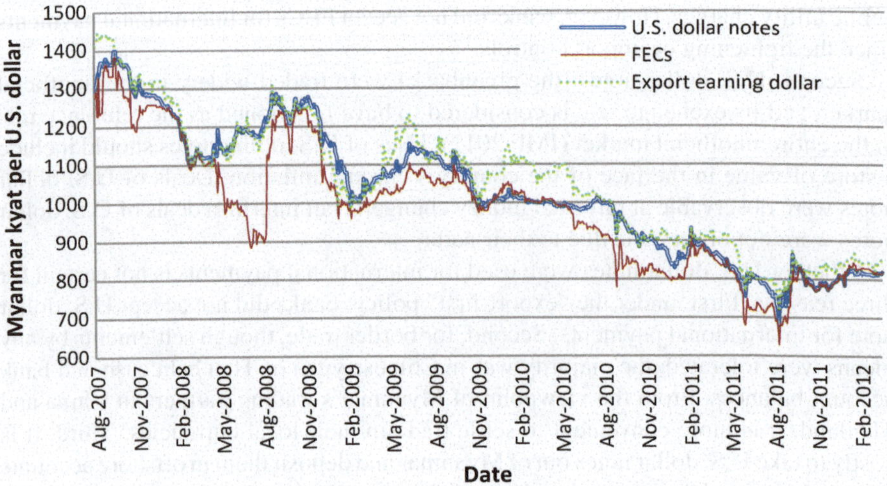

Fig. 1 Unofficial market daily exchange rates, August 15, 2007–March 29, 2012. *Source* Japan External Trade Organization (2014)

payments under strict conditions. For instance, a sudden tightening of the issuance of import licenses would reduce the demand for "export earnings" and diminish their value. In fact, for the period from October 2008 through February 2009, "export earnings" were traded at prices lower than the U.S. dollar notes. The average premium on "export earnings" for the entire observation window in Fig. 1 is 2.8%, which did not adequately compensate for the 10% export tax.

FECs were traded at a considerable discount owing to their restricted use. The average discount on FECs for the observation window is 4.4%. One episode that clearly demonstrated market segmentation was that of Cyclone Nargis and the subsequent massive inflow of the foreign aid for the disaster relief. The disaster struck the country in May 2008, causing over 100,000 fatalities. While there were large inflows of foreign aid for the disaster relief, a significant portion was disbursed in FECs, which resulted in a surge of FECs in circulation. However, because the demand for FECs was small due to their restricted use, the gap between the prices of FECs and U.S. dollar notes widened sharply to 25% in July 2008. This brought criticism from the international community, who believed the junta was profiting from the aid by manipulating the exchange rates. To stave off this criticism, the junta amended the regulations to expand the uses of FECs, including for purchases of extra-quota petroleum. Eventually, the discount on FECs fell to 1% in September 2008.

4 Informal Trade Settlement

Strict restrictions with weak enforcement stimulated informal economic activities. The private sector adapted to the restrictions on international settlements by trade settlement diversion. The U.S. economic sanctions on Myanmar in July 2008 further boosted that practice.

4.1 *Trade Settlement Diversion*

Restrictive controls on international settlements, together with the absence of trade finance facilities,[17] gave rise to the practice of trade settlement diversion. The restrictions on international settlements precluded foreign buyers' deferred payments for Myanmar's exports, and Myanmar importers' advance payments for Myanmar's imports. Private firms would lose their market if they adhered closely to the regulations. Trade settlement diversion offered a means to circumvent the restrictions.

Figure 2 illustrates how trade settlement diversion works. Here, both private exporters and importers establish a shell company in a third country, mostly in Singapore, and open an offshore bank account there under the shell company's name. In the case of Myanmar's exporters, when a foreign buyer would not agree on an advance payments, they would disguise their shell company as a foreign buyer, make the payment from that shell company's bank account to a Myanmar bank, and later receive payments from the actual foreign buyer to the shell company's bank account. By presenting evidence of a telegraphic transfer from the shell company, they were able to obtain export customs clearance at Myanmar Customs. Likewise, when a foreign supplier would not agree to deferred payments, Myanmar importers would make an advance payment from their shell company, receive the goods, and then make the payment from Myanmar to the shell company (the disguised foreign supplier) to replenish funds in the offshore account.

While trade settlement diversion provided private firms with a means to circumvent the restrictions, it imposed a heavy financial burden, which necessitated dealing in offshore account balances. Exporters needed the working capital for dummy payments from the offshore account, in addition to the working capital for procuring export commodities in the local market. Importers needed the working capital to deposit as "export earnings" FCDs at the Myanmar state banks for import license application, and working capital for advance payments from the offshore account to foreign suppliers. Firms in strained financial conditions would need to rebalance their offshore accounts and working capital at hand, which spurred them to buy and sell offshore account balances.

[17]There was no trade finance facility in Myanmar. By the conservative financial regulations, only real estate was recognized for the collateral for bank lending. In addition, for exporters, banks did not provide L/C discounting; for importers, banks issued L/Cs against the full margin only. Importers had to submit FCDs, which were frozen immediately at the issuance of L/Cs.

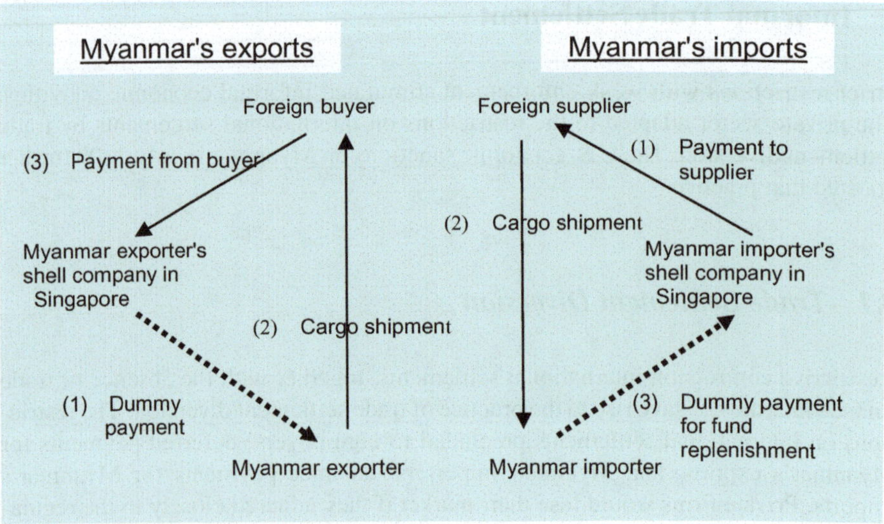

Fig. 2 Trade settlement diversion. *Source* Author

4.2 U.S. Economic Sanctions

An external factor that gave further impetus to the trade settlement diversion practice was the U.S. economic sanctions against Myanmar. Western countries initiated sanctions after Myanmar's suppression of anti-government protests and the formation of the junta regime in August and September 1988. In July 2003, the Burmese Freedom and Democracy Act banned U.S. imports from Myanmar. In July 2008, the U.S. Congress passed the Tom Lantos Block Burmese JADE (Junta's Anti-Democratic Efforts) Act, which prohibited any financial services for junta-related entities at U.S. financial institutions.

The U.S. financial sanctions of July 2008 were highly influential in their scope. In general, a sanctioning government can only forbid its citizens and corporations from engaging in specific economic activities. For instance, the U.S. general import ban was applicable only to U.S. citizens and corporations. However, the JADE Act effectively enjoined not only U.S. entities, but also third-country financial institutions from making dollar-denominated money transfers to/from Myanmar. As Fig. 3a shows, U.S. dollar-denominated payments between Myanmar and any third country usually go through a clearing system in the U.S. The figure shows the case of international money transfers from Myanmar (MFTB) to a beneficiary bank in Japan. This money transfer in U.S. dollars from Myanmar to Japan involves clearing at U.S. financial institutions which conflicts with the U.S. sanctions. Thus, the U.S. prohibition of its financial institutions from providing financial services to Myanmar companies made their trade settlements more difficult, not only with the U.S. but also with the rest of the world.

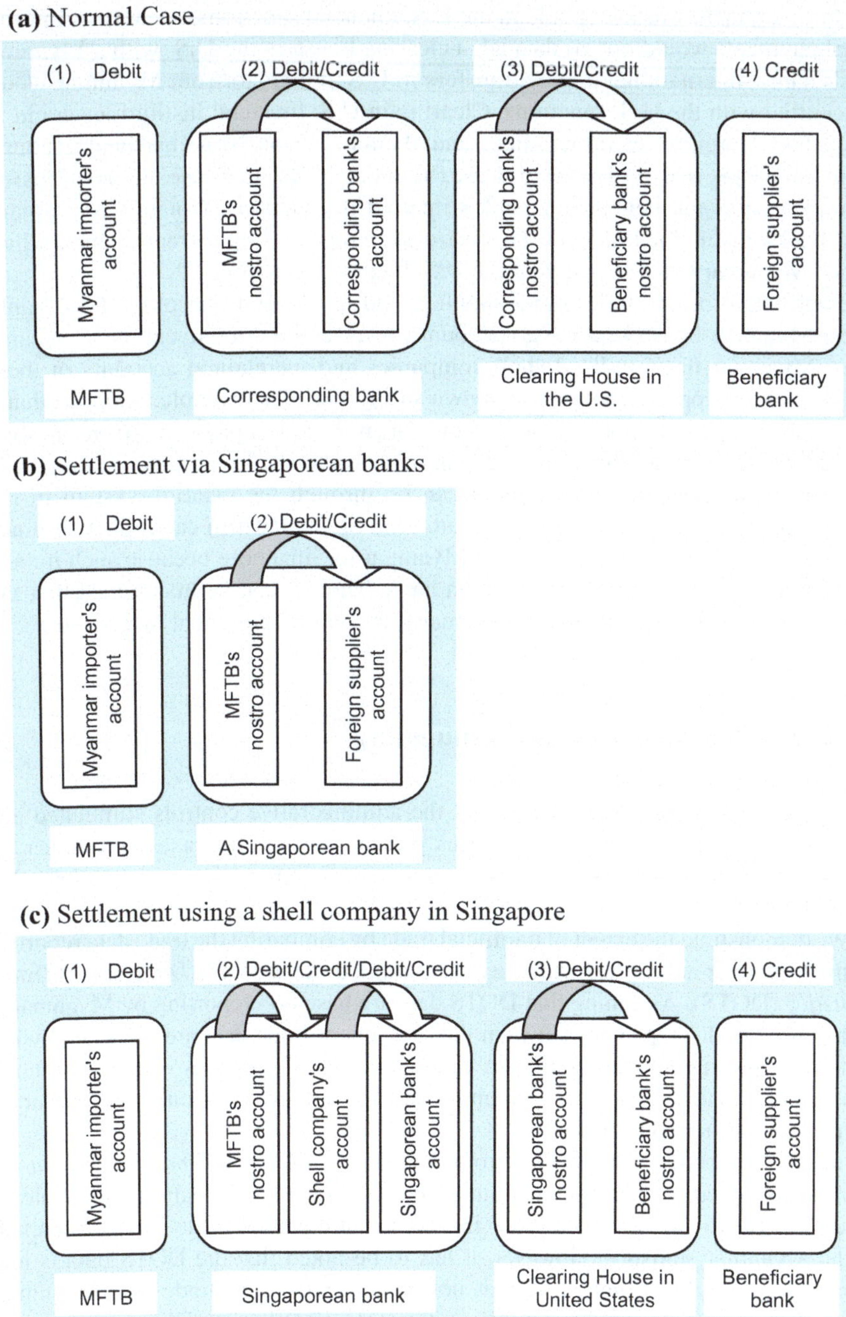

Fig. 3 Clearance of U.S. dollar-denominated money transfers. *Source* Author

However, there was a loophole in the U.S. financial sanctions. As long as international payments would not go through a clearing house in the U.S. with a Myanmar firm's name, international money transfers in U.S. dollars to/from Myanmar would not conflict with the U.S. sanctions. Clearing in U.S. financial institutions could be retrenched if foreign buyers (suppliers) and Myanmar's state banks had bank accounts in the same bank in a third country (Case (b) in Fig. 3). In such case, money transfers were cleared as the beneficiary bank's internal transactions. Notably, Myanmar's state banks maintained U.S. dollar nostro accounts in Singaporean banks, which helped Myanmar firms circumvent the U.S. financial sanctions.

Even when foreign buyers and suppliers did not have an account at the banks where Myanmar banks kept nostro accounts, firms could circumvent the U.S. sanctions. Myanmar firms utilized shell companies and maintained accounts in these banks, which is precisely the case shown in Fig. 3c. For example, suppose that a Myanmar company imports vehicles from Japan. It makes payments from its shell company's account in Singapore to Japan. Unless the shell company is recognized as a Myanmar company, its payment can go through the clearing system in the U.S. to the beneficiary's account in Japan. This Myanmar firm can replenish funds by international money transfers from Myanmar to Singapore because such money transfers complete within a Singaporean bank. Thus, it can be maintained that the U.S. economic sanctions spurred Myanmar firms' trade settlement diversion.

5 Trade Misreporting and Smuggling[18]

Other informal economic activities that the administrative controls stimulated are trade misreporting and smuggling. Firms partially evaded the taxes and duties by import under-invoicing. They skipped cumbersome import license procedures by smuggling.

We demonstrate the extent of unofficial trade by comparing the trade data reported by the Myanmar authorities with the data compiled in the IMF's *Direction of Trade Statistics* (DOTS). Assuming that DOTS data are based on reporting by Myanmar's trade partners, discrepancies between the two sets of trade data are associated with trade misreporting and smuggling. A limitation of this approach is that we ignore unofficial trade flows that were not captured by the authorities of either Myanmar or the trading partner countries.

Table 3 compares the trade data from the *Selected Monthly Economic Indicators* (SMEI) compiled by the Myanmar authorities, with the DOTS data. In this table, a ratio of SMEI to DOTS below 100% indicates that the trade value is underreported in the Myanmar statistics. However, it has to be noted that the DOTS data is not always accurate. For example, it does not include Thailand's trade with Myanmar before January 1999, which inflates the ratio of the SMEI to DOTS.

---

[18]Section 5 draws on Kubo (2012) with the kind permission of the publisher, ISEAS-Yusof Ishak Institute, http://bookshop.iseas.edu.sg.

Table 3 Trade misreporting, FY 1995–2005

Fiscal Year	1995	1996	1997	1998	1999	2000	2001	2002	2003	2004	2005
Exports (U.S. dollar, million)											
(A) Selected Monthly Economic Indicators	895	928	1,036	1,082	1,433	1,961	2,549	3,075	2,356	2,915	3,554
of which: private sector	477	605	770	745	1,109	1,380	1,333	1,653	1,308	1,262	1,603
(B) Direction of Trade Statistics	1,198	1,173	1,148	1,157	1,482	2,266	2,718	2,627	2,973	3,328	3,813
(A)/(B) (%)	74.7	79.2	90.3	93.5	96.7	86.5	93.8	117.0	79.3	87.6	93.2
Imports (U.S. dollar, million)											
(A) Selected Monthly Economic Indicators	1,832	1,993	2,309	2,702	2,605	2,321	2,734	2,297	2,235	1,979	1,982
of which: private sector	1,236	1,559	1,645	1,820	1,833	1,857	1,777	1,786	1,532	1,354	1,785
(B) Direction of Trade Statistics	2,480	2,811	2,706	2,443	2,583	2,991	2,695	2,997	3,325	3,487	3,656
(A)/(B) (%)	73.9	70.9	85.3	110.6	100.9	77.6	101.5	76.6	67.2	56.8	54.2
Private imports/Private exports (%)	259.3	257.6	213.7	244.3	165.3	134.6	133.3	108.1	117.1	107.3	111.3

Sources CSO (various issues), IMF (various issues)

According to Myanmar's official data, private sector imports reached a plateau in 1997 and then exhibited a declining trend from 2000 through 2004. These coincided with the period when the junta introduced the "export first" policy and tightened controls on imports progressively. The trade balance in the private sector was in a deep deficit until 1999, but private imports almost balanced with private exports for the period 2000–2005.

The DOTS data present a different picture, however: the country's total imports were stable until around 2001, and they then turned into steady growth. At the same time, the ratio of SMEI/DOTS for the imports declined from 110.6 in 1998 to 54.2 in 2005. These imply that the "export first" policy drove some part of the official private imports into under-invoicing and smuggling.

The ratios of SMEI/DOTS disaggregated by trading partner suggest that the proportion of unofficial trade was more prominent for the imports from neighboring China and Thailand than those from other countries. Table 4 summarizes the ratios of SMEI/DOTS for imports disaggregated by trading partner country for two periods: 2001–2005 and 2006–2010. The average SMEI/DOTS ratio for imports from Thailand in 2006–2010 was as low as 27.7 and 50.4 for China. Tight import controls might encourage import smuggling from these countries, which exploited weak controls at the land border.[19] Furthermore, the proportion of imports from China and Thailand reached 45.6% of Myanmar's total imports in 2001–2005, and it rose to 50.6% in 2006–2010.

With regard to the widening gap between the import records in SMEI and DOTS, a related question is the sources of foreign exchange used to settle the unofficial imports. Two possible sources perhaps facilitated the rise in unofficial imports. The first is private transfers redirected from the official money transfer channels to informal channels. In the Balance of Payment statistics in the appendix of this chapter, private transfers (net) peaked at USD 490 million in 1998 and declined to USD 89 million in 2002. This does not necessarily mean an actual decline in private remittances. Perhaps the "export first" policy that limited the usage of official private transfers redirected them to informal money transfers.

The second is a rise in total private transfers, including unrecorded informal flows. The number of Myanmar migrant workers in Thailand rose tremendously in this period (Kubo 2017). These workers, as of the late 2000s, were estimated to be around two million people, and the average annual remittances amounted to USD 440 per worker, totaling almost USD 1 billion. Most sent remittances through informal channels. These funds are considered to have financed payments for border trade imports and smuggling.

Trade settlement diversion can be combined with trade misreporting for tax evasion. For Myanmar's exports, suppose that the actual export price of a commodity is USD 100. An exporter disguises its shell company as a foreign buyer and sends it an invoice , undervaluing the price as USD 80. This allows the exporter to partially

[19] Kudo (2013) attributes the rise in border trade with China to the improved security in the border areas, which was previously threatened by ethnic insurgencies.

Table 4 Myanmar's imports by trading partner country, FY 2001–2005 and FY 2006–2010

Trade partner country	FY 2001–2005 average			FY 2006–2010 average		
	SMEI (USD, mil.)	DOTS (USD, mil.)	SMEI/DOTS (%)	SMEI (USD, mil.)	DOTS (USD, mil.)	SMEI/DOTS (%)
Total	2,246	3,232	69.5	4,286	7,089	60.5
China	420	916	45.8	1,270	2,520	50.4
Thailand	222	559	39.7	434	1,566	27.7
Singapore	612	632	96.8	1,150	1,065	108.0
Korea	152	178	85.7	182	361	50.3
Malaysia	212	212	100.0	179	300	59.6
Indonesia	63	70	89.9	185	253	73.1
India	92	98	94.0	174	224	77.6
Japan	198	135	147.0	216	217	99.6
Hong Kong	44	53	83.4	19	52	36.8
Germany	23	25	90.9	39	51	75.7
France	10	10	104.0	24	27	90.4
United States	38	11	334.1	45	11	421.5
United Kingdom	10	13	71.5	12	10	115.3
Others	150	320	46.9	358	433	82.6

Notes SMEI and DOTS represent *Selected Monthly Economic Indicators* and *Direction of Trade Statistics*, respectively
Sources Same as Table 3

evade the 10% export tax while receiving full payment from the actual buyer to the shell company's account. With this under-invoicing, the exporter could save USD 2 (=[USD 100 – USD 80] × 10%).

6 *Hundi*—Informal Money Transfer Operators

Smuggling and border trade, and often trade settlement diversion, relied on informal money transfers between Myanmar and offshore accounts since banks would not undertake money transfers for unofficial transactions. In general, informal money transfers in Myanmar are called *hundi*, literally meaning money transfer, and *hundi* operators offered informal money transfer services.

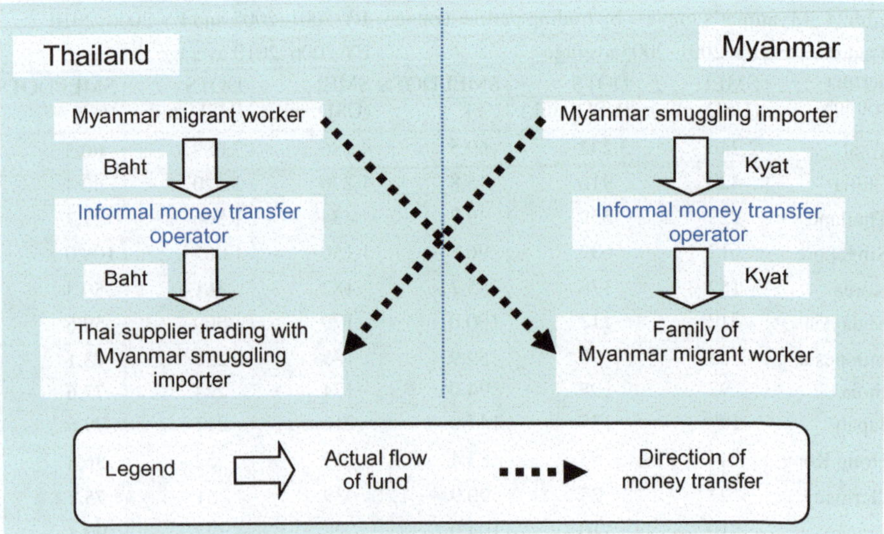

Fig. 4 *Hundi* international money transfer between Myanmar and Thailand. *Source* Author

To see how *hundi* works, Fig. 4 illustrates an example of the informal money transfer system between Myanmar and Thailand. This example has three parties: a Myanmar migrant worker in Thailand sending remittances to his family in Myanmar, a Myanmar smuggling importer who needs to pay a supplier in Thailand, and a *hundi* operator with agents in both Myanmar and Thailand. In this example, the *hundi* operator uses netting (offsetting). The Thai baht funds entrusted by the migrant worker are channeled to the Thai supplier of the smuggled goods, and the Myanmar kyat funds entrusted by the smuggling importer are channeled to the migrant worker's family. The netting simultaneously completes international money transfers and currency exchange from Thai baht to Myanmar kyat, and vice versa.

Regarding trade settlement diversion in the previous section, instead of establishing their own shell company, some private exporters and importers relied on *hundi* operators who served as a commission agent substituting for a shell company. The legal requirements for establishing a company in Singapore include hiring staff, which incurs costs on Myanmar firms to have a shell company there. Depending on the frequency and volume of transactions, it could be less costly for firms to contract with *hundi* operators than to maintain their own shell company.

Individual *hundi* operators would adjust their positions between onshore kyat balances and offshore dollar balances by swapping their liabilities with other operators in their network. For example, when one operator has excess orders of remittances from Thailand to Myanmar, while another operator has excess orders of remittances from Myanmar to Thailand, they can swap their orders. Note that this is part of the currency deals in the unofficial market.

Hundi is an efficient means of money transfers and currency exchange, especially when there is demand for money transfers for a pair in opposite directions, which allows *hundi* operators to offset transactions and offer competitive service fees. Otherwise, they need to adjust the position imbalance in some way, including a costly physical transfer of cash, which would raise fees for money transfers.

Hundi underpinned three notable money transfer corridors. The first is the Thailand–Myanmar corridor, where Myanmar migrant workers send inward remittances and Myanmar importers—either smuggling or border trade—send outward money transfers. Migrant worker remittances at least partially financed Myanmar's sizable deficit in border trade with Thailand. The second is the Singapore–Myanmar corridor, where Myanmar firms maintain offshore account balances and occasionally adjust their asset portfolios. Myanmar firms would use *hundi* to transfer working capital to their offshore accounts or to repatriate funds. Third, the China–Myanmar corridor applies to the border areas where Myanmar's exports and imports roughly balanced out. Exporters and importers exchanged Chinese yuan and Myanmar kyat directly between them or via *hundi* operators.

There has been strong complementarity between migrant worker remittances in Thailand and imports from Thailand by border trade and smuggling. On the one hand, imports from Thailand generate a massive demand for the Thai baht and informal money transfers to Thailand, which allows *hundi* operators to set competitive service fees for Myanmar migrant workers in Thailand. On the other hand, *hundi* operators' competitive fees lure the migrant workers away from formal remittance channels, making funds available for informal trade settlements.

7 Sources of Unofficial Market Persistence

We emphasize two features of Myanmar's unofficial forex market that could be associated with its persistence. First, informal deals in "export earnings" were used for official imports. Second, informal currency deals, informal money transfers, and smuggling were interconnected.

7.1 *Informal Currency Deals for Official Imports*

A unique feature of Myanmar's unofficial forex market is that foreign exchange traded outside banks were used for official imports. For normal trade, proceeds from official exports were held as "export earning" FCDs at state banks, and the junta tolerated transfers of FCDs between residents' accounts, which enabled importers to buy foreign exchange directly from exporters at free market rates. Since banks did not provide the private sector with customer dealing, informal currency deals were the sole channel for currency exchange of the official normal trade.

"Export earnings" deals outside banks could be persistent for two reasons. First, since informal deals in "export earnings" were not motivated by illegal imports, lifting restrictions on imports would not necessarily eliminate such deals. Second, as all "export earnings" deals took place outside banks, the unofficial forex market could acquire positive externality and liquidity: the more buyers and sellers that participate in informal currency deals, the easier it would be for them to find trading counterparties.

7.2 *Complementarities between Informal Currency Deals and Informal Economic Activities*

There are strong complementarities among informal deals in offshore account balances, informal money transfers, and smuggling. On the one hand, the exchange restrictions and the underdeveloped banking system deterred migrant workers abroad from sending remittances via the official channels. Their heavy use of informal money transfer operators provided a favorable environment for smuggling imports. On the other hand, weak border controls stimulated smuggling, which nourished informal money transfer operators who attracted migrant workers with competitive service fees.

While complementarity among informal activities is not unique in Myanmar, it may have been stronger than in other countries due to the country's economic environment where the boundary between legal and illegal economic activities was unclear. Smuggling flourished to circumvent the restrictions on imports. Besides, a large number of Myanmar migrant workers staying in host countries with irregular statuses did not have access to formal money transfer channels, relying on *hundi*. This environment reinforced the complementarity.

Formalization of currency exchange requires not only lifting exchange restrictions but also stringent border controls and streamlining money transfer channels for migrant workers of any status.

8 Concluding Remarks

This chapter analyzed how administrative controls shaped the unofficial forex market. The junta implemented administrative controls on the private sector to influence their use of foreign currency and to ensure repatriation of foreign exchange revenues. They had two profound impacts on the private sector. One was the segmentation of the unofficial forex market into several parts which led to multiple exchange rates within the unofficial market. The other was that they nourished informal economic activities, including trade settlement diversion and smuggling.

Because the controls differentiated the sources and influenced the uses of foreign exchange, the unofficial market was segmented into four parts dealing "export earnings" (receipts from normal trade exports), FECs, U.S. dollar notes, and offshore account balances. These four categories of foreign exchange were traded for different uses at different prices, distorting resource allocation.

The administrative controls stimulated informal economic activities, including smuggling and trade settlement diversion, both of which were underpinned by *hundi*—informal money transfer operators. Strict restrictions, but with weak enforcement, on imports and international payments drove the private sector to smuggling and trade settlement diversion.

Our analysis unveiled the diversity in informal currency deals in the unofficial forex market. On the one hand, "export earning" FCDs were traded between exporters and importers of normal trade, and they were used for official imports. On the other hand, informal deals in offshore account balances were combined with informal economic activities including smuggling and the remittances of irregular status migrant workers. As long as originating informal economic activities remain, the related informal currency deals would persist.

Appendix: Balance of Payments, FY 1995–2005 (U.S. Dollar, Million)

See Table 5.

Table 5 Balance of payments, FY 1995–2005 (U.S. dollar, million)

Fiscal year	1995	1996	1997	1998	1999	2000	2001	2002	2003	2004	2005
Trade balance	−937	−1,016	−1,280	−1,600	−1,252	−481	−251	428	541	929	1,547
Exports	895	930	1,011	1,113	1,353	1,838	2,485	2,728	2,781	2,902	3,531
Private exports	474	605	748	779	1,042	1,287	1,292	1,473	1,530	1,625	1,589
Imports	1,832	1,946	2,291	2,713	2,605	2,319	2,736	2,300	2,240	1,973	1,984
Private imports	1,209	1,498	1,627	1,818	1,824	1,855	1,778	1,794	1,523	1,361	1,369
Services (net)	60	−169	−317	178	358	207	−49	−504	−732	−808	−1,212
Receipts	402	485	554	678	573	510	466	384	270	294	320
Payments	342	654	871	500	215	303	515	889	1,002	1,102	1,532
Private transfers, net	460	457	465	490	316	203	142	89	91	130	109
Current account, excluding grants	−416	−728	−1,132	−931	−579	−71	−157	12	−100	251	444
Official grants	132	109	259	91	35	37	43	55	24	30	55
Nonmonetary capital movements	211	91	338	649	36	−59	43	−65	−28	60	−131
Long term, net	−110	−221	−81	60	−265	−265	−146	−262	−321	−194	−379
Foreign direct investment	324	316	421	592	304	208	192	191	291	251	236
Errors and omissions, net	53	−87	−64	−174	125	−161	89	−64	64	−351	−414
Overall balance	−20	−615	−599	−365	−382	−254	18	−61	−40	−10	−47

Sources IMF Country Reports (various issues)

References

Asian Development Bank (ADB). (2001). *Country economic report: Myanmar, Volume II: Statistical appendix*. Manila: Asian Development Bank.

Central Statistical Organization (CSO). (various issues). *Selected Monthly Economic Indicators*. Yangon and Nay Pyi Taw: Central Statistical Organization of the Ministry of National Planning and Economic Development.

International Monetary Fund (IMF). (various issues). *Direction of Trade Statistics CD-ROM*. Washington, DC: International Monetary Fund.

IMF. (1999). *Myanmar: Recent economic development*. IMF country report No. 99/134. Washington, DC: International Monetary Fund.

IMF. (2012). *Myanmar: Staff report for the 2011 Article IV consultation*. IMF country report 12/104. Washington, DC: International Monetary Fund.

Japan External Trade Organization (JETRO). (2014). *Daily exchange rate survey*. Unpublished material. Yangon: JETRO Yangon Office.

Kubo, K. (2012). Trade policies and trade misreporting in Myanmar. *ASEAN Economic Bulletin, 29*(2), 146–159.

Kubo, K. (2017). Evolving informal remittance methods among Myanmar migrant workers in Thailand. *Journal of the Asia Pacific Economy, 22*(3), 396–413.

Kudo, T. (2013). Myanmar's border trade with China: Roads, gates, and peace. In M. Ishida (Ed.), *Border economies in the Greater Mekong Subregion* (pp. 279–295). Hampshire: Palgrave Macmillan.

Mieno, F., & Kubo, K. (2016). Growth structure and macroeconomy under twenty years of junta regime in Myanmar. In K. Odaka (Ed.), *The Myanmar Economy: Its past, present and prospects* (pp. 51–78). Tokyo: Springer.

World Bank. (1995). *Myanmar: Policy for sustaining economic reform*. Report No. 14062-BA. Washington, DC: World Bank.

Chapter 4
Import Controls, Natural Resource Booms, and Extraordinary Real Exchange Rate Appreciation in 2007–2011

Abstract Myanmar experienced unprecedented real exchange rate appreciation in 2007–2011, while the country had two natural resource booms, one of natural gas and the other of precious stones, specifically jade. In the face of exchange restrictions, these two commodities might have affected the unofficial market rate differently. A qualitative examination of available data reveals that natural gas export revenues did not have direct impacts on the unofficial market rate, whereas jade exports were a primary cause of its extraordinary appreciation. Furthermore, tight import controls exacerbated the appreciation by blocking outlets for large inflows of export revenues in the unofficial forex market. While bringing in exchange rate instability temporarily, the relaxation of exchange restrictions since 2011 is expected to restore the self-stabilizing feature of exchange rates.

Keywords Natural resource boom · Real exchange rate · Currency appreciation Myanmar

1 Introduction

During the junta's rule in 1988–2011, the Myanmar kyat exchange rate fluctuated sharply in the unofficial forex market. Until mid-2007, the kyat depreciated continuously in nominal terms, which was followed by the extraordinary appreciation in both nominal and real terms. The nominal exchange rate of the kyat *vis-à-vis* the U.S. dollar appreciated from above 1300 kyats per U.S. dollar in September 2007 to 740 kyats in August 2011. Taking into account Myanmar's much higher inflation than its trade partner countries, the real exchange rate appreciated more steeply than the nominal exchange rate.

The extraordinary appreciation coincided with natural resource booms—sharp increases in exports of natural gas and jade. The country's total exports increased more than threefold from USD 2.8 billion in 2004 to USD 8.8 billion in 2010.

This chapter draws on Kubo (2013) with the permission of the publisher, John Wiley and Sons.

K. Kubo, *Myanmar's Foreign Exchange Market*,
https://doi.org/10.1007/978-981-13-1789-7_4

Together, these two commodities accounted for more than half of the country's total exports in 2010.

We investigate how exchange restrictions complicated and amplified the impacts of resource booms on the unofficial exchange rate. We take into consideration two points. First, as far as administrative controls held back the export receipts in one segment of the segmented forex market, such export revenues would not affect the exchange rates in the other segments. Second, as the International Monetary Fund (IMF) argues, tight import controls exacerbated the appreciation since they curtailed demand for foreign exchange (IMF 2012).

This chapter aims to shed light on the relationship between exchange restrictions and the extraordinary currency appreciation. The remainder of this chapter is structured as follows. Section 2 overviews the trends of exchange rates, external balance, and the composition of exports. Section 3 offers a brief review of the related literature on exchange rate dynamics, with particular attention to natural resource booms. Section 4 examines the relationship between the real exchange rate appreciation and the two resource booms, taking into account the forex market segmentation. Section 5 illustrates how the lifting of exchange restrictions since 2011 unleashed pent-up demand for imports and unraveled the real exchange rate appreciation, which is supportive evidence that exchange restrictions had exacerbated the appreciation. Section 6 summarizes the analysis and offers some concluding remarks. In the rest of this chapter, unless otherwise mentioned, exchange rates refer to those in the unofficial forex market, not the official exchange rate.

2 Trends in Exchange Rates and External Balance

This section overviews the trends of nominal and real exchange rates. It then illustrates the trend of the balance of payments and the composition of exports.

2.1 Exchange Rate Trends

Myanmar experienced unstable macroeconomic conditions for over two decades. The government routinely monetized fiscal deficit, and an excess supply of base money led to high inflation in the medium- to long-term (Turnell 2011). In the short term, the consumer price index (CPI) exhibited sharp swings, which were partially attributable to the volatile price of rice, the main staple of the country. Figure 1 illustrates changes in the retail rice price, CPI, and the nominal exchange rate of the kyat per U.S. dollar. The junta restricted rice exports tightly, putting them under the state monopoly. Due to the ban on private exports of rice, a good harvest in 2000 led to a sharp fall in the domestic price, and a lean harvest to a rise in subsequent years. The average CPI inflation rate for the period from January 1998 through March 2012 was 21.0% per annum.

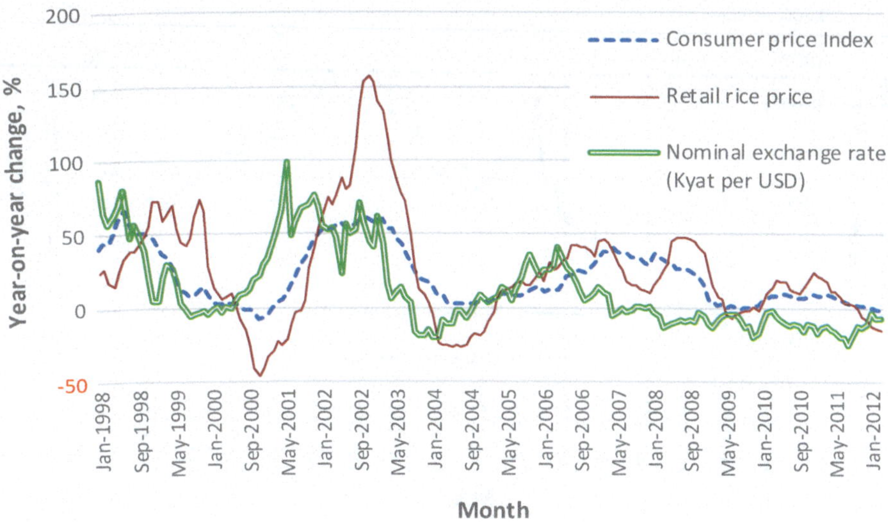

Fig. 1 Year-on-year changes in consumer price index, retail rice price, and unofficial nominal exchange rate, January 1998–March 2012. *Sources* International Financial Statistics, CD-ROM; Central Statistical Organization (CSO) (various issues); Japan External Trade Organization (JETRO) (2014)

Regarding the trends of exchange rates in the medium- to long-term, Fig. 2 depicts the exchange rates of the Myanmar kyat *vis-à-vis* the U.S. dollar in nominal and real terms. The real exchange rate is calculated as the product of the nominal exchange rate (the kyat *vis-à-vis* the U.S. dollar) and the ratio of the U.S. CPI to the Myanmar CPI. In this figure, the twelve-month average of the real exchange rate for the base year of 1997 is set at 100. Its fall, say from 100 to 90, indicates a real appreciation of the kyat.

The figure shows that the nominal exchange rate depreciated steadily until 2007. The chronic nominal depreciation had mostly been accompanied by CPI inflation with some time lags, which leveled the real exchange rate. The real exchange rate appreciated temporarily by nearly 50% from 1997 to early 2000s and reverted to the initial level in 2003.

However, an extraordinary real appreciation started in 2007 and continued until 2011. In this figure, the real exchange rate was 134 in April 2006, and it plunged to 41 in December 2011. This indicates that the value of the U.S. dollar in terms of Myanmar's consumption bundle diminished to one third in five years.[1] Figure 1 shows that year-on-year changes in the nominal exchange rate were negative throughout the period from 2007, whereas the CPI inflation rate remained above zero during the same period.

[1] The U.S. dollar weakened against major currencies in this period, which partly accounted for the appreciation of the kyat. However, the kyat appreciated far more sharply than other currencies in the region.

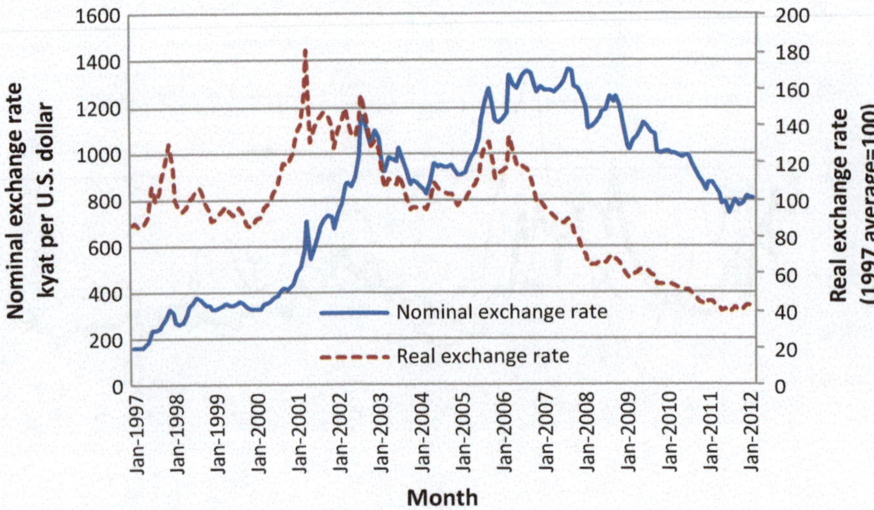

Fig. 2 Exchange rates of Myanmar kyat vis-à-vis U.S. dollar, January 1997–March 2012. *Sources* Same as Fig. 4.1

Although there is a concern about the credibility of data for Myanmar's CPI, the issue is unlikely to be a reason for this extraordinary real appreciation. In April 2009, the authorities switched the base year for calculation of CPI from 1997 to 2006, which coincided with a fall in the annual inflation rate from double to single digits. Thus, the inflation rate may be underestimated for the period from 2009 onward. However, a higher inflation rate, if such occurred, would have resulted in a more acute appreciation of the real exchange rate.

2.2 *External Balance and Composition of Exports*

Natural gas exploration brought about one of the most significant changes to Myanmar's external balance in the 2000s. With the exploration of gas fields by foreign investment, natural gas exports through the pipeline to Thailand was started in 1998. Full-scale production and exports were achieved by 2002. Table 1 depicts the trend of natural gas exports, along with the total exports and imports by sector (state and private sectors). Natural gas exports have been entirely registered as state sector exports. These were nil until 1997 but rose to USD 1,015 million in 2004 and USD 3,493 million in 2011, equivalent to 35% and 38% of the country's total exports in the respective years.

When we consider the effect of natural gas exports to the balance of payments, however, we have to be aware that a significant portion of the revenues was surrendered to foreign stakeholders that had mining concessions. For example, against the

Table 1 Trade by ownership, FY 2000–2011

Fiscal year	Private sector		Public sector			Total	
	Imports	Exports	Imports	Exports		Imports	Exports
				Total	Of which natural gas		
Unit: US dollar, million							
2000	1,857	1,380	463	581	171	2,321	1,961
2001	1,777	1,333	958	1,216	632	2,734	2,549
2002	1,786	1,653	511	1,422	912	2,297	3,075
2003	1,532	1,308	703	1,048	580	2,235	2,356
2004	1,354	1,262	626	1,653	1,015	1,979	2,915
2005	1,368	1,603	614	1,951	1,073	1,982	3,554
2006	1,804	2,068	1,125	3,155	2,031	2,928	5,223
2007	2,443	2,369	903	4,044	2,532	3,347	6,413
2008	2,592	2,480	1,971	4,313	2,384	4,563	6,793
2009	2,806	3,087	1,381	4,443	2,906	4,186	7,530
2010	4,623	3,502	1,781	5,354	2,515	6,404	8,856
2011	6,611	4,073	2,421	5,056	3,493	9,032	9,129

Note Selected Monthly Economic Indicators report the trade value in kyat. This is converted into U.S. dollars using the official exchange rate. *Source* CSO (various issues)

natural gas exports of USD 2,906 million in 2009, the balance of payments statistics recorded USD 1,776 million of income (debit), which mostly corresponded to such payments to the foreign stakeholders. Income (debit) is a component of the current account.

Apart from natural gas, there has been another resource boom in jade. A state economic enterprise (SEE)—the Myanma Gems Enterprise, under the Ministry of Mines—organized gem emporiums in the country either twice or three times a year, attracting foreign buyers especially from China. While the organizer was an SEE, sellers were private businesses. The junta labeled the sales at emporiums as "export earnings" and imposed a 10% export tax.

Jade exports jumped from USD 234 million in 2005 to USD 647 million in 2007, and further to USD 2,017 million in 2010.[2] Figure 3 summarizes the trend of exports by commodity. The share of jade in the country's total exports reached 23% in 2010. The bulk of the jade exports were to China. In 2011, China imposed special duties on these jade imports, which depressed Myanmar's exports to USD 41 million in the official figure.

[2]Egreteau (2012) attributes the rapid increase in jade exports to the entry of powerful business cronies into the extraction and trading of jade in the second half of the 2000s. Jade extraction is capital intensive.

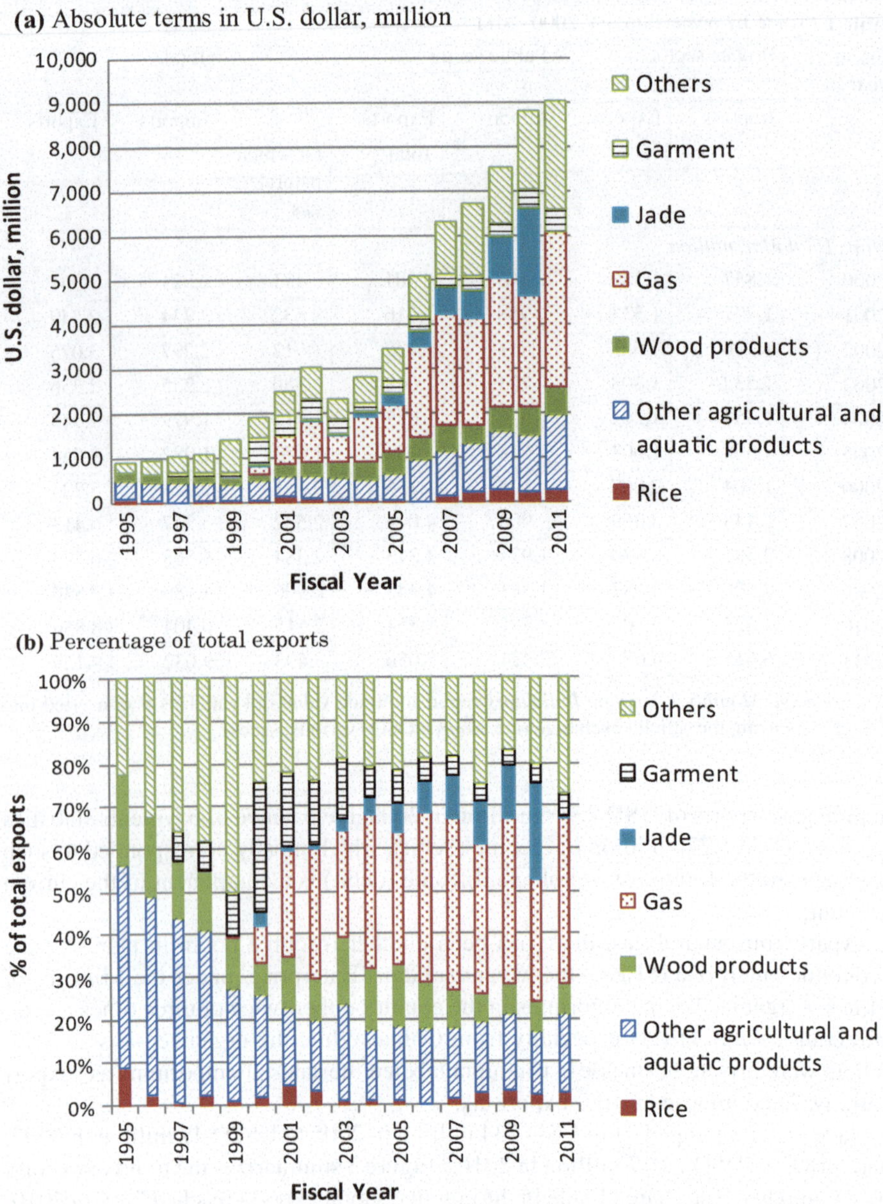

Fig. 3 Structure of Myanmar's exports, FY 1995–2011. *Note* Prior to 2000, jade exports are included in "Others." *Source* CSO (various issues)

Among the primary commodities that held large shares in Myanmar's exports, some belonged to the state sector and the others to the private sector. Exports of natural gas and wood products (teak and hardwood) belonged to the state sector. Rice exports were under the state monopoly until 2007. Traditional export commodities of the private sector were beans and pulses, whose main destination was India; others included aquatic products, garments, and jade.

Exports of manufactured goods, which often use imported raw materials and intermediate goods, were stagnant, perhaps due to tight import controls. The garment industry was one of few exceptions. The export-oriented garment sector emerged in the early 2000s, using the consignment production scheme, whereby Myanmar factories only undertook processing for fees, and foreign buyers consigned textiles and purchased all sewn clothes. In this scheme, the authorities allowed license-free imports of textiles on condition that all sewn clothes were exported. This scheme facilitated private firms to bypass exchange restrictions. However, when the United States, the leading destination of the country's garment exports, imposed a total ban on imports of Myanmar goods as a means of economic sanctions in July 2003, the export-oriented industry lost momentum (Kudo 2008). This eventually prompted a concentration of the country's exports in natural resources.

The trend of the external balance was influenced by the resource booms. Figure 4 summarizes selected indices of the balance of payments. The current account balance had been in deficit before the rise in natural gas exports turned it to surplus in 2002. The current account balance fell in deficit again in 2008 partially due to the continued increase in global fuel prices. The government used to monopolize the fuel imports and distribute fuel by the quota system at subsidized prices. As the global fuel prices increased, the government loosened the grip and allowed its cronies to import fuel in 2008, which led to a rise in fuel imports from USD 370 million (2007) to USD 586 million (2008), and further to USD 1,391 million (2010).[3]

Figure 4 also indicates that Myanmar's overall balance turned positive in 2006 and remained in surplus during 2006–2010, which is attributable to foreign direct investment (FDI) in the resource sectors. Although the current account balance turned to negative in 2008, the capital account surplus—FDI in the resource sectors, including mining, natural gas exploration, and hydropower generation—made up for it. Such FDI brought foreign exchange income to the government including concession fees.

The private sector was insulated from the FDI in the resource sectors. The FDI which was related to the private sector included manufacturing, and hotels and tourism, which was much smaller than the government-related FDI in the resource sector. The total amount of FDI permitted for the period 2008–2009 amounted to USD 1,314 million, of which the manufacturing sector accounted for USD 6 million and the hotel and touring sector USD 27 million while the bulk of FDI went to the mining sector (USD 858 million) and the oil and gas sector (USD 393 million).[4] We have to be aware that, given the segmentation of the forex market, changes in the balance of payments and the exchange rate were not always linked.

---

[3] However, full liberalization of fuel imports by the private sector did not take place until the new government took office in March 2011.

[4] These figures are retrieved from CSO (various issues).

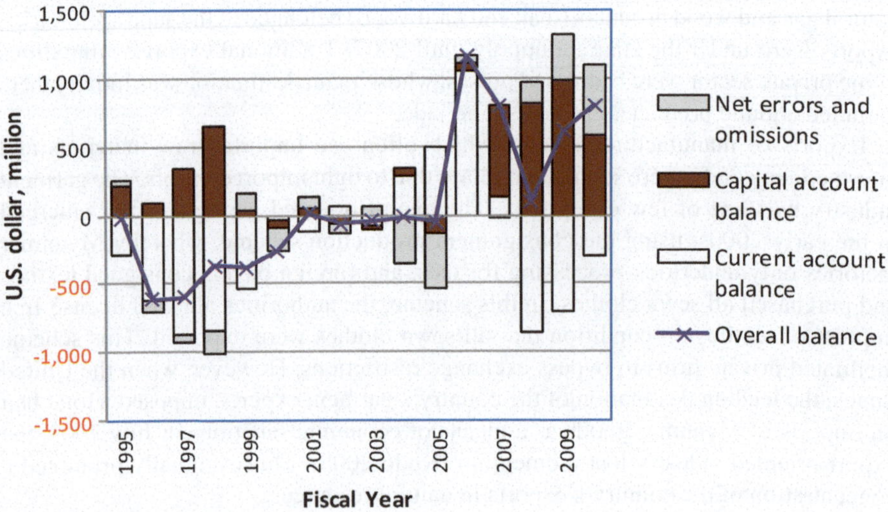

Fig. 4 Balance of payments, FY 1995–2010. *Source* International Financial Statistics CD-ROM

3 Determinants of the Real Exchange Rate

We briefly review the literature on exchange rate dynamics, with particular attention to the relationships of the real exchange rate with (i) an excess supply of base money and (ii) a natural resource boom.

3.1 Money Supply

We ask if an excess supply of base money leads to an appreciation of the real exchange rate. It brings in inflation and raises the domestic CPI. Besides, it causes a nominal depreciation of the local currency against foreign currencies when the exchange rate regime is a floating one. With regard to Myanmar, the unofficial market rate is de facto independently floating. As far as changes in nominal exchange rate and CPI inflation cancel out, an excess supply of base money does not lead to real exchange rate appreciation.

However, such neutrality of money on the real exchange rate often does not hold. Price controls exist in many economies, and prices often exhibit stickiness. Differences in responses of the CPI and the nominal exchange rate to monetary shocks result in fluctuations in the real exchange rate, at least in the short run. In the literature of real exchange rates, the neutrality of money supply on the real exchange rate, or purchasing power parity in general, remains inconclusive (Sarno and Taylor 2002).

Nonetheless, it is argued that purchasing power parity hold more in high-inflation countries, as price adjustment occurs more quickly (Froot and Rogoff 1995). With regard to Myanmar, a time series data analysis by Kubo (2007) found a cointegration relationship among the money supply, the CPI, and the nominal exchange rate, for the period from 1996 through mid-2006. This implies that the real exchange rate was mean-reverting in that period.

3.2 *Resource Boom*

We next consider the impact of a resource boom on the real exchange rate. For instance, in oil-exporting countries, a hike in oil prices in the international market brings about a rise in export revenues. As far as the incremental export revenues are spent on imports, this does not exert any effect on the nominal or real exchange rate.[5] There are two potential channels by which a resource boom exerts impacts on the real exchange rate.

First, exchange of the export revenues to the domestic currency raises the demand for the domestic currency, increasing the price of the domestic currency in terms of foreign currency. This translates to a nominal exchange rate appreciation, and *ceteris paribus* leads to a real exchange rate appreciation.

Second, as a part of the export revenues exchanged to the domestic currency is spent on non-tradable goods, their prices move up as well. A resulting rise in prices of non-tradable goods reinforces the real exchange rate appreciation. Corden (1984) calls this the "spending effect" of a natural resource boom.

Thus, a natural resource boom is associated with an appreciation of the real exchange rate through these two channels. Named after the experience in the Netherlands, a real exchange rate appreciation and a resulting decline in traditional export industries due to a natural resource boom are called the "Dutch disease."[6]

4 Sources of Real Exchange Rate Appreciation

On the basis of the structure of the foreign exchange market as laid out in Chaps. 2 and 3, we investigate causes of the real exchange rate appreciation, as well as factors that have amplified the appreciation.

---

[5] When there are import controls, this does not hold. Here, a baseline case where there are no import controls is presumed.

[6] The "Dutch disease" refers to the decline of the traditional export sector due to a resource boom (Corden 1984). For recent literature surveys on the "Dutch disease," see Magud and Sosa (2010), and van der Ploeg (2011).

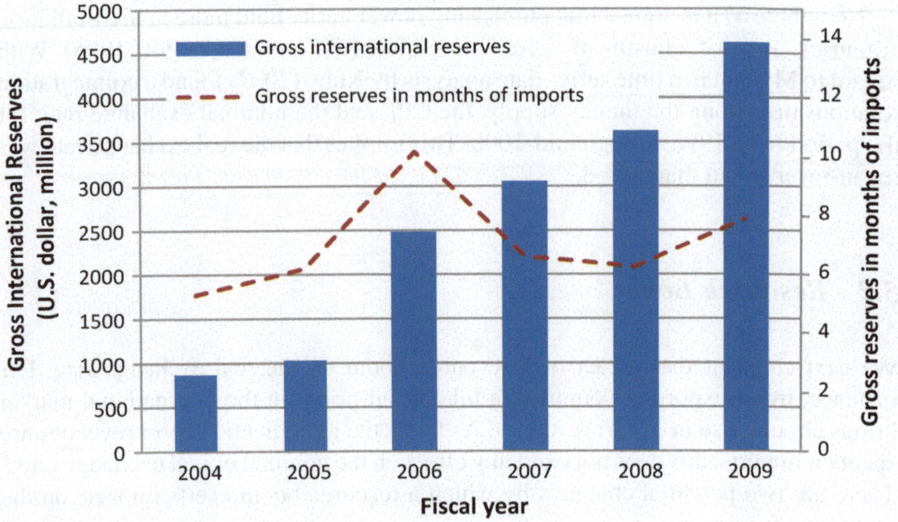

Fig. 5 International reserves (gross official reserves), FY 2004–2009. *Sources* IMF Country Report (various issues)

4.1 *Linkage between the Two Resource Booms and Currency Appreciation*

Although natural gas exports certainly improved the balance of payments, their impact on the unofficial forex market is not so clear. The natural gas export revenues flowed to the state sector. As shown in Table 1, the state sector was in a large trade surplus from 2002. Under the foreign exchange management described in Chap. 2, however, there was no channel by which foreign exchange could flow from the state sector to the unofficial forex market. As far as export revenues remained in the state sector, they should not exert direct impacts on the unofficial forex market.

The international reserves increased sharply, which is consistent with our conjecture that natural gas export revenues did not channel to the unofficial forex market. Figure 5 illustrates the trend of gross international reserves. With the rise in natural gas exports, gross international reserves built up rapidly, especially in 2006. We consider that the government shelved a considerable portion of natural gas export revenues as foreign currency deposits (FCDs) in the Myanma Foreign Trade Bank (MFTB), which led to a surge in international reserves.[7]

[7] The definition of international reserves appears to be amended in 2011. Before 2011, FCDs at the MFTB seem to have been counted as international reserves. After the amendment of the definition, the amount of international reserves in 2009 revaluated from USD 4,638 million to USD 2,809 million. Figure 5 is consistently compiled based on the previous valuation method, which allows us to see the trends of foreign asset accumulation. However, this figure is not consistent with Fig. 2 in Chap. 5.

Neither should the spending effect of natural gas export revenues have triggered a real exchange rate appreciation. The junta had valuated the foreign currency revenues at the official exchange rate. For instance, when the official and unofficial market rates are 5.5 kyats and 800 kyats per U.S. dollar, respectively, this practice undervalues the foreign currency surplus in terms of the kyat by less than one hundredth (1/100). Thus, the natural gas exports could hardly contribute to the state budget in terms of the local currency. We argue that the dual exchange rate system functioned to prevent the natural gas exports from exacerbating the real appreciation.

There could be an indirect impact on the unofficial market if rising export revenues in the state sector alleviated its crowding-out effect on private sector imports. When the state sector had been short of foreign exchange, it might have procured imported goods from the private sector, which might have crowded out the private sector's imports. The natural gas export revenues might have alleviated such crowding-out, which might add to the appreciation of the kyat.[8] Due to data limitation, however, we are not able to test this hypothesis.

By contrast, jade exports are a more likely cause of the appreciation in the unofficial forex market. Jade exports brought "export earnings" to the private sector. The trend of jade exports overlapped more closely with the exchange rate trend. Table 1 shows that the private sector exports hit USD 2 billion for the first time in 2006. The proportion of jade exports to total private sector exports increased from 14.6% in 2005 to 27.3% in 2007 and 57.6% in 2010.

There are two anecdotes about the relationship between the kyat appreciation and jade exports. First, business people in Yangon ascribed the kyat appreciation to the "Jade disease."[9] Second, in an article, Myanmar's renowned economist U Myint, who was later appointed as the chief economic advisor to President Thein Sein, recommended that the authorities reduce the number of gem emporiums in order to alleviate the currency appreciation (Myint 2011).

4.2 *Other Factors behind Currency Appreciation*

There are three other factors that possibly exacerbated the kyat appreciation. First, the IMF (2012) points to the exchange restrictions as a factor that amplified the appreciation. Restrictive controls on imports blocked outlets for large inflows of foreign exchange from natural resource exports. Without such restrictions, a real exchange rate appreciation would have stimulated imports, since it would make imported goods cheaper. A rise in imports would then have alleviated the real appreciation. Usually, a foreign exchange market has such a self-stabilizing feature, thus preventing the

[8] Supporting evidence of subsiding crowding-out is that by April 2005, the authorities abolished the import license conditionality that had required applicants to allocate 80% of the total import value for goods on the priority list.

[9] Author's interview with an executive committee member of the Union of Myanmar Federation of Chambers of Commerce and Industry in March 2012.

exchange rate from changing in one direction for a sustained period. Myanmar's administrative controls undermined this self-stabilization feature. Table 1 in Sect. 2 shows that private sector imports increased only gradually in 2002–2008.[10] The trade balance of the private sector turned to balance or surplus from deep deficit in the 1990s.[11]

The second factor is the regulatory change in the exchange restrictions in January 2010, wherein the authorities extended the definition of "export earnings" eligible for import licenses; migrant worker remittances and foreign currency incomes from services, including local hotels which charged foreigners in the U.S. dollar, began to be labeled as "export earnings." This policy change expanded the stock of foreign exchange usable for official normal trade imports. It might partly account for the continued appreciation of the kyat despite sizable trade deficits in the private sector in 2010 and 2011. Table 1 shows that trade deficits of the private sector reached USD 1.1 billion in 2010 and USD 2.5 billion in 2011.

Third, one more factor underlying appreciation was the soaring demand for the kyat. There were massive sales of state properties in February 2011 just before the end of the junta's regime. These are regarded as transfers of state assets by the junta to its allies. While the exact figures are not available, the scale of the sales is considered to be unprecedented. Moreover, the settlements of asset purchases had to be in kyats. The deadline for the settlements was August 2011, which coincided with a sharp fall in the nominal exchange rate to 740 kyats per U.S. dollar. This was the lowest since February 2002. It is conjectured that there were massive portfolio reallocations away from foreign-currency-denominated assets, which furthered the appreciation.

5 Lifting of Exchange Restrictions since 2011

Relaxation of import controls was followed by a surge in private imports and a depreciation of the kyat in the unofficial forex market. This can be interpreted as side evidence that the tight import controls had exacerbated the appreciation.

5.1 Import Liberalization and Kyat Depreciation

The concern about the currency appreciation subsided as the kyat started to depreciate in 2012. The nominal exchange rate depreciated from around 800 kyats per U.S. dollar in December 2011 to above 1300 kyats in December 2015.

---

[10]There are considerable discrepancies between Myanmar's official data—*Selected Monthly Economic Indicators*—and the data compiled by the IMF (See Table 3 in Chap. 3). Focusing on trading of "export earning," we proceed the analysis in this section drawing on the official data.

[11]The rise in private imports in 2008–2011 was due to loosening of the state monopoly of fuel imports as explained in Sect. 2.2 of this chapter.

This depreciation took place simultaneously with rapid growth in private sector imports. The private sector imports more than doubled from USD 6,609 million in 2011 to USD 14,023 million in 2015 according to Myanmar's official statistics. The mirror statistics of Myanmar's trading partner countries indicate that the country's total imports increased from USD 14,702 million in 2011 to USD 23,858 million in 2015,[12] implying that the rise in official private imports was not only attributable to a shift from unofficial to official imports, but also to a net increase in total private imports.

One of the underlying factors of the sharp rise in imports was the relaxation of exchange restrictions.[13] First, the new government abandoned the state monopoly and distribution of fuel and liberalized private imports of fuel in 2011. Fuel imports surged from USD 1,391 million (2010) to USD 1,927 million (2011). Second, relaxing the tight control on vehicle imports, the new government introduced the car substitution program in September 2011, which allowed owners of old models to import a newer model for replacement. Japanese used cars have accounted for the bulk of Myanmar's car imports. The number of imports of used passenger cars from Japan increased from 4,935 in 2010 to 37,797 in 2011 and 91,797 in 2012.[14] Japan's exports of vehicles to Myanmar amounted to USD 57 million in 2010 and jumped to USD 934 million in 2012. Third, the authorities abolished the "export-first" policy in April 2012, which we will examine in more detail in Chap. 5. While private sector exports grew steadily, the growth of private sector imports by far exceeded them.

The release of pent-up demand for imports after easing of exchange restrictions naturally brought in the kyat depreciation. Myanmar's per capita import in 2015 was USD 466, which was considerably lower than those of the peers in the region such as Cambodia, for which the corresponding figure was USD 1,239.[15] There is ample room for growth in private sector imports due to pent-up demand, which would bring in a further adjustment in the real exchange rate.

---

[12]The mirror statistics indicate that Myanmar's exports soared in 2014. This was mainly owing to China's jade imports. China Customs reported that jade imports from Myanmar jumped to USD 11.6 billion in 2014 from a five-year average of USD 0.6 billion in 2009–2013. Such a rise in China's jade imports is not consistent with Myanmar's official data. It might represent a once-off adjustment in China's import statistics.

[13]Another factor is the rise of FDI and the associated imports by foreign firms.

[14]According to Myanmar's official statistics, the *Selected Monthly Economic Indicators*, the number of imported passenger cars in 2012 (flow) was equivalent to 27.8% of the country's total registered passenger cars (stock), indicating enormous pent-up demand during the period of strict controls on car imports.

[15]These figures are calculated with data in Asian Development Bank's *Key Indicators for Asia and the Pacific 2016*.

5.2 *Implications of the Appreciation Episode*

We argue that, in the face of large inflows of foreign exchange from jade exports to the unofficial forex market, tight import controls undermined the self-stabilization of the exchange rate. The lifting of the exchange restrictions since 2011 unleashed pent-up demand for imports and partially restored the exchange rate self-stabilization. In terms of the real exchange rate of the kyat *vis-à-vis* the U.S. dollar, it depreciated by approximately 31% from 41 in December 2007 to 54 in December 2015. Despite the sizable nominal depreciation from 800 kyats per U.S. dollar to 1300 kyats, the real exchange rate remained fairly appreciated, partly due to high inflation in the country.

The kyat is expected to depreciate in both nominal and real terms during the reform period. As long as the economy undergoes structural reforms that change the relative demand for and supply of foreign exchange, the exchange rate will exhibit temporary instability. Nevertheless, the reforms are conducive to restoring the self-stabilizing feature of the exchange rate in the medium to long run.

6 Concluding Remarks

The unofficial market rate exhibited an extraordinary appreciation in the period 2007–2011, which coincided with two natural resource booms—natural gas and jade. The purchasing power of the U.S. dollar in Myanmar diminished to one-third of its previous level in the five-year period. This chapter investigated the relationship between the real exchange rate appreciation and the natural resource booms, taking into account the peculiar structure of the forex market under the exchange restrictions.

The exchange restrictions complicated the relationships between the unofficial market exchange rate and the two resource booms. Revenues from natural gas exports were confined within the state sector, so they could not be a direct cause of the appreciation in the unofficial forex market. By contrast, revenues from jade exports belonged to the private sector, labeled as "export earnings," which would change the balance between supply and demand of foreign exchange in the unofficial forex market.

Furthermore, the exchange restrictions exacerbated the appreciation, as they blocked outlets for large inflows of jade export revenues in the unofficial forex market. While relaxation of exchange restrictions since 2011 has weakened the kyat vis-à-vis the U.S. dollar, it is expected to restore the self-stabilizing feature of the exchange rate.

References

Central Statistical Organization (CSO). (various issues). *Selected Monthly Economic Indicators*. Nay Pyi Taw: Central Statistical Organization of the Ministry of National Planning and Economic Development.

Corden, W. M. (1984). Booming sector and Dutch disease economics: survey and consolidation. *Oxford Economic Papers, 36*(3), 358–380.

Egreteau, R. (2012). The Burmese jade trail: transnational networks, China and the (relative) impact of international sanctions on Myanmar's gems. In N. Cheesman, M. Skidmore, & T. Wilson (Eds) *Myanmar's Transition: Openings, Obstacles and Opportunities* (pp. 89–116). Singapore: Institute of Southeast Asian Studies.

Froot, K. A., & Rogoff, K. (1995). Perspectives on PPP and long-run real exchange rates. *Handbook of International Economics, 3,* 1647–1688.

IMF (International Monetary Fund). (various issues). *International Financial Statistics* CD-ROM. Washington, DC: International Monetary Fund.

IMF (2012). Myanmar: staff report for the 2011 Article IV consultation. IMF Country Report No. 12/104. Washington, DC: International Monetary Fund.

Japan External Trade Organization (JETRO). (2014). *Daily exchange rate survey*. Unpublished material. Yangon: JETRO Yangon Office.

Kubo, K. (2007). Determinants of parallel exchange rate in Myanmar. *ASEAN Economic Bulletin, 24*(3), 289–304.

Kubo, K. (2013). Real exchange rate appreciation, resource boom, and policy reform in Myanmar. *Asian-Pacific Economic Literature, 27*(1), 110–126.

Kudo, T. (2008). The impact of U.S. sanctions on the Myanmar garment industry. *Asian Survey 48*(6), 997–1017.

Magud, N., & Sosa, S. (2010). When and why worry about real exchange rate appreciation?: the missing link between Dutch disease and growth. IMF Working Paper WP/10/271. Washington, DC: International Monetary Fund.

Myint, U. (2011). Myanmar kyat exchange rate issue. Paper presented at National Workshop on Reforms for Economic Development of Myanmar, Nay Pyi Taw, August 19–21, 2011.

van der Ploeg, F. (2011). Natural resources: curse or blessing. *Journal of Economic Literature, 49*(2), 366–420.

Sarno, L., & Taylor, M.P. (2002). Purchasing power parity and the real exchange rate. *IMF Staff Papers, 49*(1), 65–105.

Turnell, S. (2011). Fundamentals of Myanmar's macroeconomy: a political economy perspective. *Asian Economic Policy Review, 6*(1), 136–153.

Chapter 5
Foreign Exchange Market Reform since 2011: Linkage between the Official and Unofficial Markets

Abstract Foreign exchange policy reform since 2011 has undergone highly visible changes. One is exchange rate unification in a move to a managed float. Another is the licensing of authorized dealer banks and their customer dealing, wherein private exporters and importers can officially avail themselves of currency exchange. Nonetheless, low turnover in the official market suggests prevalent informal currency deals. To see the linkage between the newly launched official market and the unofficial market, we evaluate the impact of the official foreign exchange auction on the unofficial exchange rate using a GARCH model. Empirical results imply that the foreign exchange auction as an intervention instrument has only modest impacts on the unofficial market, despite its considerable costs in terms of the central bank's international reserves.

Keywords Exchange rate unification · Unofficial forex market · Managed float
Foreign exchange auction · Myanmar

1 Introduction

Since the political transition from the junta to a democratic government in March 2011, extensive reforms pertinent to the forex market have been implemented. The Central Bank of Myanmar (CBM) abolished the official peg of the Myanmar kyat to the special drawing right (SDR) of the International Monetary Fund (IMF) in April 2012 and moved to a managed float comprising the daily foreign exchange auction. The official rate in terms of kyats per U.S. dollar was devalued from 5.561 kyats at the end of March 2012 to 818 kyats on April 2, 2012. Private banks, licensed as foreign exchange dealers, have been offering customer dealing with private firms and

This chapter draws heavily on Kubo (2014, 2017) with the kind permission of the publishers, ISEAS-Yusof Ishak Institute, http://bookshop.iseas.edu.sg; Taylor & Francis Ltd, http://www.tandfonline.com.

K. Kubo, *Myanmar's Foreign Exchange Market*,
https://doi.org/10.1007/978-981-13-1789-7_5

individuals since July 2012. The "export-first" policy was also lifted in April 2012, followed by the redemption of foreign exchange certificates (FECs) in July 2013.

In contrast to visible changes in the forex market structure, impacts of the reforms on the unofficial forex market are not evident. Have the reforms contained informal currency deals? Has the CBM acquired the capacity to influence the unofficial market rate and reduce its fluctuations?

This chapter examines the linkage between the newly launched official market and the unofficial market. In particular, the efficacy of foreign exchange auctions in smoothing out exchange rate fluctuations is evaluated. The remainder of this chapter is structured as follows. Section 2 outlines the reforms pertinent to the forex market. Section 3 describes the linkage between the official and the unofficial forex markets. Section 4 presents an empirical analysis about the impacts of auctions on the unofficial forex market. Specifically, a generalized autoregressive conditional heteroscedasticity (GARCH) model is employed to see if the forex auction could reduce exchange rate volatility. Section 5 presents concluding remarks.

2 Outline of Reforms since 2011

This section outlines the reforms pertinent to the forex market since 2011 and illustrates how they shape the official forex market. This is the first step towards understanding the linkage between the official and the unofficial forex markets.

2.1 *Forex Market Reform*

Major changes in the foreign exchange policies include (i) issuance of money changer and foreign exchange dealer licenses, (ii) introduction of a managed float with foreign exchange auctions, (iii) redemption of FECs, and (iv) lifting of controls on international trade.

2.1.1 Chronology

In October 2011, the official foreign exchange counter was reopened on Thein Phyu Road in Yangon, operated by 17 private banks that received money changer licenses from the CBM. At the counter, authorized money changer banks exchanged U.S. dollar notes for Myanmar kyats at prices close to the prevailing unofficial market rates.[1] Despite the official peg of the Myanmar kyat to the SDR still being in place at that time, the new government officially recognized the unofficial market rates.

[1] It is not clear how the prices of foreign exchange were determined at the Thein Phyu counter.

The Thein Phyu exchange counter was intended for retail transactions in cash. Purchases of foreign currency for imports were basically prohibited, except for the car substitution program (IMF 2012: 5).[2] Moreover, caps were set on the amount of foreign exchange a customer could either sell or buy per transaction. Initially, the cap was set at USD 2,000, or the equivalent in Singapore dollars and euros, per transaction, and it was raised to USD 10,000 in January 2012. Moneychanger banks at the counter often set their caps lower than the statutory one, due to the limited availability of foreign exchange and kyat cash in their hands. Later, the foreign exchange counters expanded outside the Thein Phyu counter.

In November 2011, the CBM granted foreign exchange dealer licenses to 11 private banks.[3] Different from money changer license holders, authorized dealer banks were allowed both to make current international transactions, including international payments, and to accept foreign currency deposits (FCDs). The CBM did not activate their licenses immediately. Besides, regardless of Myanmar's banking regulations, banks were not able to undertake international settlements without nostro accounts at banks in foreign countries. Since July 2012, four private banks have successively started accepting FCDs and undertaking international settlements. This has terminated the state banks' monopoly on international banking. Customer dealing by private banks opened a channel for private exporters and importers to convert currencies officially.

In April 2012, the CBM abolished the official peg of the Myanmar kyat to the SDR and moved to a managed float, and it simultaneously commenced daily two-way multiple-price auctions of the U.S. dollar (IMF 2013b). The CBM calls for both bids (CBM sales) and offers (CBM purchases) of foreign exchange from authorized dealer banks. At every auction, the CBM presents a cut-off rate in terms of kyats per U.S. dollar and accepts those bids (offers) above (below) the cut-off rate. The CBM announces to the public the cut-off rate as the official reference rate.

The functions of Myanmar's forex auction are threefold. First, in the auction, the CBM retrieves a market-based exchange rate, which is labeled as the official reference rate. The CBM regulates authorized money changers to set their buying and selling rates within $\pm 0.8\%$ of the official reference rate. Second, it provides a facility for authorized dealer banks to adjust their foreign exchange positions. Third, it equips the CBM with a means to intervene in the forex market.

Regarding trade policies, another significant change came in April 2012, when the Ministry of Commerce abolished the "export-first" policy. Corresponding to this decision, the CBM issued an instruction that banks[4] should treat any foreign

---

[2] In September 2011, the government eased the restrictions on car imports. With the car substitution program, individuals who owned a certain old model were permitted to import a newer model for replacement. This policy resulted in a car import boom.

[3] As of November 2011, there were 19 private banks. Those banks that did not obtain authorized dealer licenses were mostly small banks whose paid-up capital did not fulfill the requirement for the license. In August 2012, three additional private banks obtained authorized dealer licenses.

[4] Initially, this instruction was applied only to the state banks, the Myanma Foreign Trade Bank and the Myanma Investment and Commercial Bank, as none of the private banks engaged in current international transactions until July 2012.

exchange, whether FCDs of official export earnings or not, equally for current international transactions. This policy change signifies that authorized dealer banks accept foreign exchange originating from any sources for settlement of normal trade imports.

In December 2012, the CBM commenced granting money changer licenses to non-bank private firms. The existing unofficial money changers, as well as new entrants, have joined the official market. The authorized money changers must comply with the regulation that restricts their buying and selling exchange rates within the band prescribed by the CBM.

In March 2013, the CBM announced redemption of FECs. The CBM ensured that FECs would be exchanged at both state and private banks for either U.S. dollar notes, FCDs, kyat cash, or kyat deposits. FECs in circulation as of December 2012 were reportedly USD 31 million, equivalent to 0.04 months of Myanmar's imports in 2012.

Finally, in August 2013, interdealer trading of foreign exchange among authorized dealer banks was instituted under the guidance of the CBM. The CBM provided technical assistance for authorized dealer banks to trade foreign currency among themselves. It is expected that a deep and liquid interbank forex market will take over two functions of the foreign exchange auction which are retrieval of a market-based official exchange rate and a facility for authorized dealer banks to adjust foreign exchange positions.

2.1.2 Evaluation

A notable drawback of the forex market reforms lies in the state sector. Despite the introduction of the managed float, state economic enterprises (SEEs) and the state sector are still insulated from the private sector. While a reform of the state budget system is underway, the centralized foreign exchange administration in the state sector remains. For example, the Myanma Oil and Gas Enterprise, the top foreign exchange earner SEE, surrenders its export revenues to the state budget. A segmentation of the forex market thus remains between the state budget system and the private sector.

Nonetheless, a remarkable change in the state sector is that the administrative exchange rate for the fiscal accounting of foreign currency transactions was devalued to 820 kyats per U.S. dollar for the first half of the fiscal year 2012 and 860 kyats for the second half—values that were close to the unofficial market rates.[5] This change allowed the government to assess the financial viability of individual SEEs.

With regard to the private sector, the devaluation of the official exchange rate per se was mostly irrelevant,[6] because all foreign currency transactions in the private

[5]The information in this paragraph is based on the author's interview with the Ministry of Finance and Revenue, Myanmar, in February 2013.

[6]There were some indirect impacts on the private sector. For example, the devaluation could lead to a rise in import duties payable in the kyat. For evaluation of import duties, however, the government had used an administrative exchange rate, which had been close to the unofficial rate.

sector had been taking place at unofficial market rates. Figure 1 depicts the trends in exchange rates for U.S. dollar notes, FECs, and "export-earning" FCDs for the period from April 1, 2011, to March 30, 2013. There were no sharp changes in the unofficial exchange rates during a couple of months either before or after the abolition of the official peg in April 2012.

More importantly, the reform largely unified the exchange rates within the unofficial forex market. The abolition of the "export-first" policy led to a convergence of prices for various categories of foreign exchange. Figure 1 shows that three exchange rates converged in mid-May 2012, following the abolition of the "export-first" policy in April 2012. It is worth noting that the resolution of market segmentation by May 2012 facilitated subsequent redemption of FECs in July 2013.

The abolition of the "export-first" policy, in addition to the relaxation of import controls, is an essential step for Myanmar to remove all restrictions on payments and transfers for current international transactions and to eliminate multiple exchange rates (multiple currency practices). These are the obligations that the IMF sets out for its member countries, including Myanmar, in Article VIII of its *Articles of Agreement* to promote world trade. According to the IMF (2014), Myanmar is yet to remove restrictions on remittances for invisible transactions (such as remittances of profits by foreign firms); thus, Myanmar is classified as a country in the transitional arrangement status of Article XIV. The new government intends to remove the remaining restrictions and accept Article VIII obligations.

Furthermore, the authorities have been paving the way for an official two-tier forex market in the private sector. Authorized dealer banks utilize daily auctions and the interbank forex market to adjust their foreign exchange positions, which constitutes

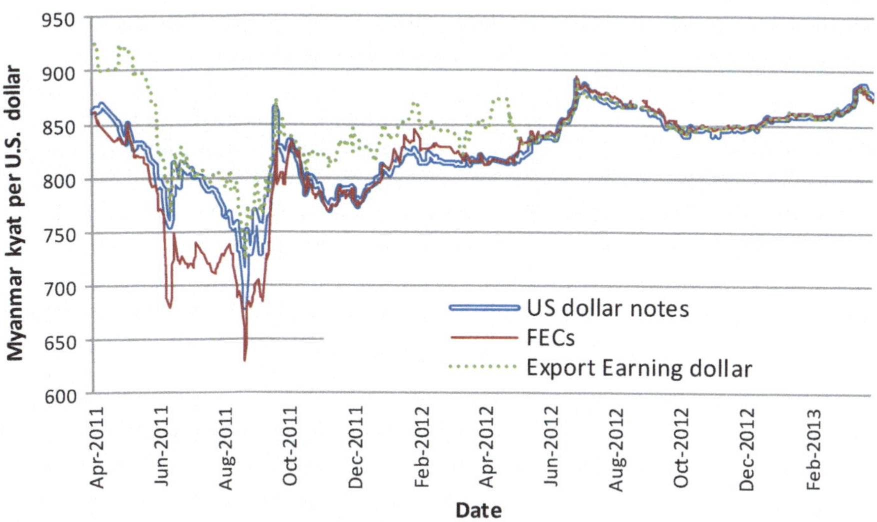

Fig. 1 Daily exchange rates in the unofficial forex market, April 1, 2011–March 30, 2013. *Note* FEC refers to foreign exchange certificate. *Source* Japan External Trade Organization (2014)

the wholesale market.[7] These authorized dealer banks engage in customer dealing with private exporters and importers for their current international transactions, which constitutes the retail market.

2.2 *Reform of the Central Bank and the Financial Market*

The formal financial market, including the interbank lending market and the market of local currency-denominated assets, is complementary to the official forex market. As presented in Chap. 1, a modern forex market is comprised of interbank deals of financial derivatives, such as swaps and forward contracts. Interbank deals of financial derivatives, in turn, require the interbank lending market and the securities market for the following reasons. First, for interbank deals of foreign exchange, as there is the settlement risk, banks have to evaluate the credit risk of counterparties. The interbank lending market is a sufficient condition for this. Second, since banks set the forward exchange rates and swap rates based on the interest rate parity condition, forward and swap deals require a liquid market of local currency-denominated assets with a benchmark yield curve. The modern forex market develops in tandem with the formal financial market.

Towards the development of the financial market, there have been comprehensive reforms concerning the Central Bank. Prior to the reform, the Central Bank was affiliated with the Ministry of Finance and Revenue (MoFR) under the 1990 Central Bank Law. The governor of the CBM was ranked as director-general of the MoFR. The CBM routinely accepted Treasury Bills of the Union Government at the directed interest rate. In fact, there had been no Treasury Department in the MoFR before the amendment of the Central Bank law, and the CBM served as the treasury of the Union Government, which led to chronic monetization of fiscal deficits.

The amendatory law, which was promulgated in July 2013, mandates the CBM to concentrate on price stability. Under the amendatory law, the governor and members of the board of directors are appointed by the President of the Republic with the approval of the national parliament. The new law states that the position of governor is a minister-level post. In parallel with the amendment of the CBM's mandate, the Treasury Department was newly established within the MoFR. The reform has separated the CBM from the MoFR.

Since January 2015, Treasury Bills have been sold through auctions. The MoFR issues Treasury Bills with maturities of three, six, and twelve months. In the auction, banks participate as competitive bidders, whereas the CBM is the non-competitive bidder that accepts unsold Treasury Bills at a price determined by the successful bids. The Treasury Bills' auction is considered to alleviate monetization of fiscal deficit

[7]Strictly speaking, the amount of bids and offers that an authorized dealer bank can place in an auction is limited in accordance with the deposits that it maintains in the CBM. The banking regulations also impose a limit on a bank's net open position within 30% of its paid-up capital.

partially. In September 2016, the new government commenced auctions of Treasury Bonds that had maturities of two, three, and five years.

Apart from the autonomy of the CBM from the Union Government, two significant developments are expected to pave the way for the CBM to conduct monetary and exchange rate policies. One is the introduction of deposit auctions in September 2012, and the other is the accumulation of international reserves at the CBM.

First, the deposit auction is a potential policy instrument for the CBM to manage the money supply.[8] The auctioned deposit is an instrument similar to central bank securities to absorb excess liquidities of commercial banks. As the CBM pursues reserve money targeting as its monetary policy framework, the CBM intends to utilize deposit auctions to absorb liquidities and to sterilize forex market interventions. The maturities of the auctioned deposits are one, two, four, and six weeks. In contrast with the daily foreign exchange auctions, the deposit auctions are held mostly every two weeks.

Combined with the Treasury Bills auction, the deposit auction is also expected to function as a means of price discovery. A market-based short-term interest rate in deposit auctions and medium-term interest rate in Treasury Bills auction could constitute a benchmark yield curve in Myanmar's nascent financial market.

However, these securities' auctions have not functioned well. Private banks—major players in Myanmar's nascent financial market—have barely participated in these auctions, for at least two reasons. One reason is the state-owned Myanma Economic Bank (MEB), which bids low interest rates at deposit auctions due to its excess liquidity[9] (IMF 2014). The other is weak financial supervision and weak enforcement of the statutory reserve requirement on banks; even when banks failed to fulfill the reserve requirement, which was 10 percent of deposits, they were, reportedly, not always charged penalties.[10] This deters banks from holding liquid financial assets for liquidity management. As a result, the deposit auction and Treasury Bills auction have been dominated by the MEB, and the interest rate outcomes are not considered to represent a benchmark yield curve. The absence of a benchmark yield curve arrests the development of the financial market.

Second, with regard to international reserves, the reform plan included the transfer of the reserve management function from the Myanma Foreign Trade Bank (MFTB) to the CBM. Before the reform, foreign currency revenues of the state sector had been maintained as FCDs at the MFTB. In 2012, there were large transfers of foreign assets from the MFTB to the CBM. Figure 2 shows the trend in international reserves. It indicates that USD 2 billion of international reserves were transferred in 2012.

[8]Along with deposit auctions, credit auctions—a kind of central bank lending facility—were designed, but they have never been implemented.

[9]Its excess liquidity might be due to low lending capacity.

[10]In April 2016, the CBM cut the reserve requirement ratio to 5% from 10%, while narrowing the definition of reserves. Before this amendment, 75% of reserves could be held in interest-bearing Treasury bonds, although that portion of the reserve had to be deposited at the CBM. After the amendment, all of the reserves must be kyat cash deposited at the CBM. This change in the definition of reserves is expected to help the stringent implementation of bank supervision.

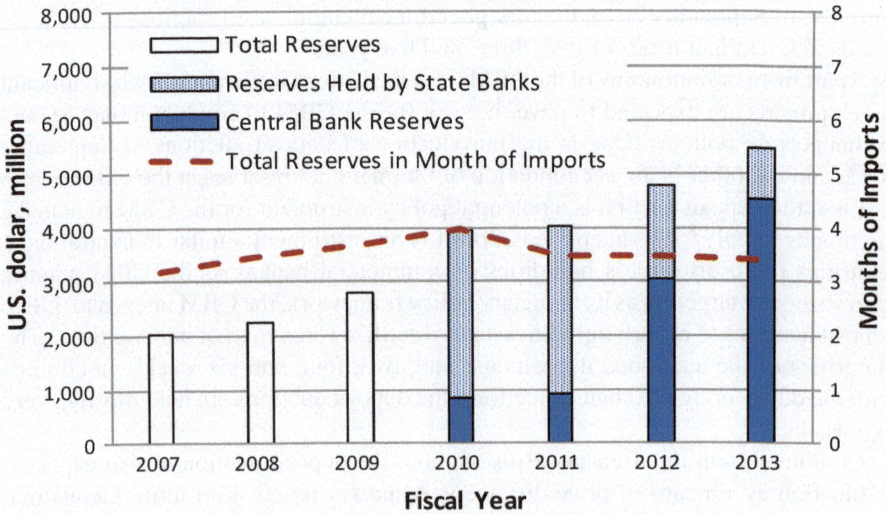

Fig. 2 International reserves, FY 2007–2013. *Note* Total reserves are the sum of the reserves held by state banks and the Central Bank. Disaggregated data on reserves for 2007–2009 are not available to the author. *Sources* IMF Country Report (various issues)

Adequate international reserves would equip the CBM with a cushion to smooth out exchange rate fluctuations.

Another development in the financial system is entries of foreign banks. The CBM issued provisional licenses for nine foreign banks to open branches in October 2014.[11] Since April 2015, some of these banks have opened branches and begun operations in Myanmar. However, the CBM has been heavily restricting the operations of foreign banks, which discourages their demand for local currency assets and their foreign exchange deals with local banks. Foreign banks are yet to add to the development of the financial and the forex markets.

3 Linkage between the Official and Unofficial Forex Markets

This section describes the linkage between the official and the unofficial forex markets. Specifically, it illustrates the scale of the official forex market and the functions of foreign exchange auctions as a market intervention instrument.

[11]In the second round of foreign bank licensing, another four banks won the provisional licenses in March 2016.

Table 1 Official forex market and private sector international trade, January 2014–December 2014

	Monthly average (USD, million)	Ratio to private exports
Wholesale		
Auction turnover[a]	155.7	0.39
(Central bank sales, gross)	65.5	0.16
(Central bank purchases, gross)	90.2	0.22
Interbank dealing turnover	17.5	0.04
Retail		
Customer dealing turnover	110.2	0.27
Memorandum items		
Private exports	401.5	1.00
Private imports	1131.7	2.82

[a]Monthly average for September 2013–August 2014. *Sources* Central Bank of Myanmar website; Central Statistical Organization (various issues)

3.1 *Scale of the Official Forex Market*

How large are auctions and the official market in comparison with the unofficial market? The official forex market is composed of the wholesale section (the auction and the interbank market) and the retail section (the customer dealing of authorized dealer banks). Table 1 compares the turnover of the wholesale and retail sections of the official market with the amount of private exports in 2014. Since the size of the unofficial market is not observable, we use the export amount as a yardstick. We refer to private sector exports because the state sector had not yet sold and bought foreign exchange in the market; it was confined to the administrative foreign exchange allocation system. The auction turnover and the customer dealing turnover include both sales and purchases of foreign exchange by authorized dealer banks. The table shows that the ratio of the customer dealing turnover to the private exports in 2014 was as low as 0.27, implying prevalent informal currency deals wherein private exporters sold export receipts directly to private importers.[12]

Concerning the wholesale section of the official market, the interbank dealing turnover has been as low as 4% of the private exports, whereas the auction turnover has been relatively high. Inactive interbank trading is possibly associated with the fact that authorized dealer banks either had similar foreign exchange positions with each other or did not have credit lines with each other, or both. Regarding auctions, as will be shown in the next subsection, CBM sales and purchases of foreign exchange were more unbalanced than the average figures in Table 1 imply. In some months, there were almost no sales of foreign exchange, while there were almost no purchases in other months.

[12]A firm that undertook both exports and imports would manage foreign exchange within itself. Such a firm would not enter either the official or unofficial forex market.

Finally, the table indicates a considerable gap between the exports and imports of the private sector. This gap raises the question of how the trade deficit was financed. During the period of the "export-first" policy, private exports and imports were more or less balanced. A sizable trade deficit in the private sector in 2014 suggests that "export earnings" were not a primary source of foreign currency for the private sector imports. First, a part of the private imports might belong to foreign-invested firms; foreign direct investment (FDI) in kind shall be included as private imports while they do not accompany payments from Myanmar. FDI in kind would add to the gap between the private exports and imports. Second, a part of the foreign exchange that banks purchased from the CBM at auctions might be channeled to private imports. However, customer dealing turnover has been as low as 4% of private exports in 2014, so that the forex flows from the CBM to the banks would not account for a significant portion of the trade deficits. Third, a considerable part of the private imports was through cross-border trade, which was settled either in cash or through the informal *hundi* money transfer system (Chap. 3). Therefore, a part of the private sector trade deficit was possibly financed by migrant worker remittances through the informal channels. How the trade deficit was financed remains a subject for further investigation.

3.2 Auctions and the Unofficial Market

Figure 3 summarizes the foreign exchange auction's daily records for the period April 2012–September 2014, along with the trends in the official reference rate and the prevailing unofficial market rate. In this figure, a negative value of the Central Bank net purchase indicates that the CBM sold U.S. dollars to authorized dealer banks.

There are two notable tendencies in auctions. First, successful bids and offers by participating banks are concentrated on one side, either the CBM's sales or purchases of U.S. dollars, for some prolonged periods. In several months in 2012, there were no sales of foreign exchange by the CBM. In 601 working days of our sample period, there were only 132 days where the CBM had both sales and purchases of U.S. dollars in the auctions. On 246 days, the CBM accepted bids (dollar sale) only, and on 189 days offers (dollar purchase) only. These are consistent with the view that the foreign exchange positions of individual banks were similar to each other, which was also one of the reasons for inactive interbank deals.

Second, gaps between the official reference rate and the unofficial market rate widen occasionally. Compared with the unofficial exchange rate, the official rate overvalued the Myanmar kyat by more than 4% in June 2013, while the official rate also undervalued the kyat by 2% in September 2012. The official rate overvaluing the Myanmar kyat stimulated private banks' bids (e.g., CBM sales of dollars), as in June 2013, whereas the undervaluing official rate brought in private banks' offers (e.g., CBM purchase of dollar), as in September 2012.

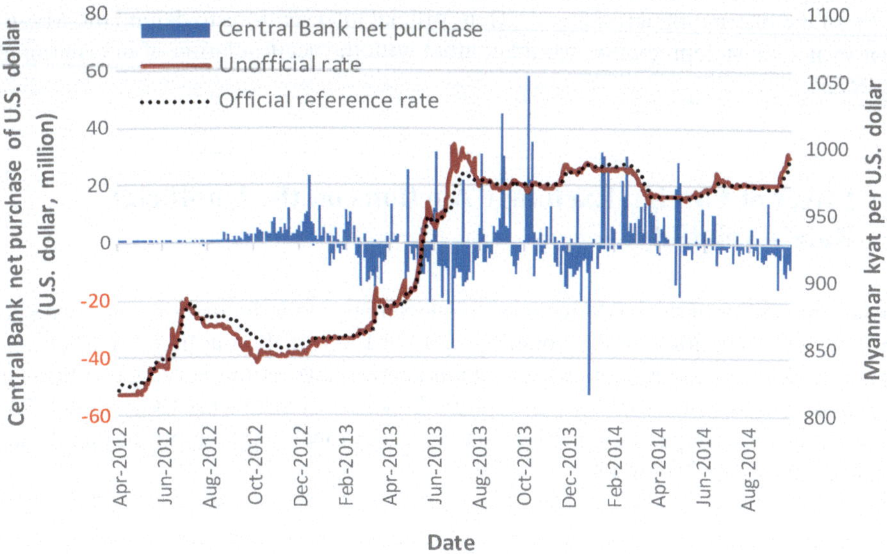

Fig. 3 Daily foreign exchange auction, April 2, 2012–September 25, 2014. *Sources* Central Bank of Myanmar; e-trade Myanmar

Occasional wide gaps between the official and unofficial rates can be interpreted as the CBM's attempt to smooth out fluctuations in the unofficial exchange rate. The gaps have tended to widen following abrupt changes in the unofficial exchange rate. When the kyat strengthened against the U.S. dollar sharply in the unofficial market, the CBM purchased dollars with a more depreciated exchange rate, as in July 2012. Likewise, when the unofficial rate depreciated sharply, the CBM sold dollars with a more appreciated exchange rate, as in July 2013. The IMF (2013a: 7) concludes that the CBM has sought to smooth out exchange rate fluctuations without targeting either a specific level or range.

Another interpretation of the gaps between the official and unofficial rates is that authorized dealer banks' arbitrage trading exploited the auctions. The banks' successful offers (bids) of foreign exchange were concentrated on days when the reference rate was higher (lower) than were the prevailing unofficial market rates. The banks could obtain a windfall gain by buying foreign currency from the CBM in the auction at an appreciated exchange rate and selling it for the kyat in the unofficial market. This casts doubt over whether the banks used the auction as a facility to adjust their foreign exchange positions.

Furthermore, one of the auction's critical negative impacts is drains on international reserves. As the foreign exchange auctions are two-way, they can lead to either accumulation or dissipation of international reserves. In March 2013, the monthly sales and purchases of international exchange by the CBM were USD 145.3 million and USD 5.5 million, respectively. Net drains of USD 139.8 million amounted to

4.7% of the international reserves.[13] Thus, official interventions to defend the Myanmar kyat against depreciation would conflict with the accumulation of international reserves.

4 Effect of Foreign Exchange Auctions on the Unofficial Rate's Volatility

To see the ability of the CBM to smooth out exchange rate fluctuations, we evaluate the impact of auctions on the volatility and the level of the unofficial market rate changes. When changes in the unofficial market rate have a time-varying conditional variance structure of errors, we can capture the volatility with a GARCH model. We then analyze the impacts of auctions on the conditional variance of unofficial rate changes in a GARCH model.

4.1 Data

The variables we utilize in this analysis are the unofficial market rate and daily foreign exchange net purchases by the CBM through auctions. For the unofficial rate, we use the informal dealers' selling price of U.S. dollar notes at the closing of the market in the afternoon, disseminated by a private market information service company.[14] The auction data are obtained from one of the private banks. The sample period spans April 2, 2012, to September 25, 2014.[15] The total number of observations is 601.

For the unofficial market rate, we define the daily return of the U.S. dollar against the Myanmar kyat as follows:

$$r_t \equiv 100 \times \left[\ln(BLK_t) - \ln(BLK_{t-1})\right], \tag{1}$$

which is proximate to the percentage change in the prevailing unofficial market rate, BLK_t. A positive r_t value indicates depreciation of the kyat against the U.S. dollar. Figure 4 depicts the daily return of the U.S. dollar. As is common for financial variables, volatility clustering is observable; large changes in the unofficial rate were followed by large changes, and small changes by small changes. The figure indicates that the daily return of the unofficial market rate has a time-varying conditional variance structure of the errors.

[13] According to the IMF (2014: 22), the Central Bank's international reserves as of the end of March 2013 were USD 3,062 million.

[14] e-Trade Myanmar Co. Ltd. (http://etrademyanmar.net/newetm/home).

[15] It is extended from the sample period of Kubo (2017) by one year.

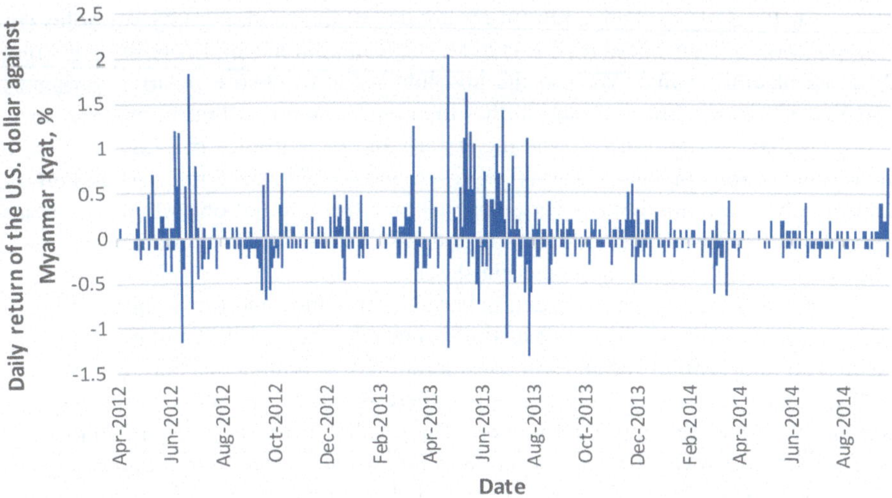

Fig. 4 Daily return to the U.S. dollar in the unofficial forex market, April 2, 2012–September 25, 2014. *Source* e-trade Myanmar

4.2 *Empirical Model*

Following Baillie and Bollerslev (1989), Dominguez (1998), and Edison et al. (2006), among others, we analyze impacts of the foreign exchange auctions on the unofficial market rate returns using a GARCH model. With regard to the benchmark model, we consider two factors. First, as in Edison et al. (2006), we take into account day of the week effects, if any, on the exchange rate return, based on the assumption that the exchange rate is more volatile on Mondays. Second, we consider possible asymmetric effects of good news and bad news; depreciation shocks would have more persistent effects on the exchange rate than would appreciation shocks.

To the benchmark model, we add a term representing the CBM's net purchases of foreign exchange through the daily auctions in both the conditional mean and conditional variance equations. In particular, the specification of the model is as follows:

$$r_t = \varphi_0 + \varphi_1 r_{t-1} + \sum_{i=2}^{5} \varphi_i D_{it} + \varphi_6 I_t + \varepsilon_t \tag{2}$$

$$\varepsilon_t | \Omega_{t-1} \sim \mathrm{N}(0, \sigma_t^2) \tag{3}$$

$$\sigma_t^2 = \delta_1 + \sum_{i=2}^{5} \delta_i D_{it} + \delta_6 |I_t| + \alpha_1 \varepsilon_{t-1}^2 + \alpha_2 Dum_{t-1} \varepsilon_{t-1}^2 + \beta \sigma_{t-1}^2 \tag{4}$$

where r_t is the daily exchange return; D_{it} are day of the week dummy variables (for example, $D_{2t} = 1$ on Tuesdays); I_t is the CBM's net purchase of foreign exchange; $|I_t|$ is its absolute value. We use the absolute value to ensure positive variances. Equation (3) shows our assumption that the conditional distribution of error terms ε_t is a normal distribution with the mean zero and the variance σ_t^2. Equation (4) is the variance equation, where α and β represent the ARCH effect and GARCH effect, respectively. Dum_t are dummy variables that take the value of one when $\varepsilon_t < 0$ and zero otherwise. Therefore, α_1 refers to the ARCH effect of a depreciation shock, while $\alpha_1 + \alpha_2$ is that of an appreciation shock.

When incorporating the intervention variables into the conditional mean and variance equations, some studies, such as Baillie and Osterberg (1997) and Broto (2013), use lagged intervention variables in consideration of simultaneous bias. For the case of Myanmar's foreign exchange auctions, there is a time lag between intervention and the closing of the unofficial market. The results of the auctions are announced at around 10:00 AM. The data on the unofficial market rate is the market's afternoon closing price. Therefore, endogeneity is less of a concern compared with the abovementioned studies.

The parameters of interest are φ_6, which measures the impact of the foreign exchange auction on the level of the unofficial market rate return, and δ_6, which measures the impact on the variance of changes in the unofficial market rate return. We expect $\varphi_6 > 0$, as CBM's foreign exchange purchase will lead to a depreciation of the Myanmar kyat *vis-à-vis* the U.S. dollar. Regarding the unofficial market rate's volatility, if the auctions as official interventions smooth out unofficial market rate fluctuations, the sign of δ_6 will be negative.

4.3 *Empirical Results*

Table 2 reports the results of estimation. Model (1) is the baseline model without intervention (auctions) terms. Model (2) is with the CBM's net purchase of foreign exchange in the conditional mean and conditional variance equations. The estimated coefficients fulfill the sufficient conditions for well-defined variance and covariance, which are $\alpha_i > 0,\ \beta > 0,\ and \sum \alpha_i + \beta < 1$. For the diagnostics of standardized residuals, the Ljung–Box *Q*-statistic tests for serial correlation indicate that the null hypothesis of no serial correlation in residuals cannot be rejected. The ARCH Lagrange multiplier test is also carried out to ensure that the GARCH models correct heteroscedasticity.

With regard to the variance equation of the baseline Model (1), the coefficient on the dummy variable for appreciation shocks is not significant, implying that the impacts of good news and bad news on exchange rate volatility are not asymmetric. On the other hand, the coefficients on day of the week dummies are all negative and statistically significant in the variance equation. This indicates that the exchange rate was more volatile on Mondays than any other day of the week.

Table 2 GARCH model regression results

Model	(1)		(2)	
Mean equation				
Constant	0.007	(0.812)	−0.0176	(0.479)
r_{t-1}	0.0191	(0.660)	0.0037	(0.938)
Tue	−0.0065	(0.846)	0.0245	(0.409)
Wed	0.0268	(0.472)	0.0374	(0.242)
Thu	0.0203	(0.554)	0.0543**	(0.046)
Fri	−0.0086	(0.802)	0.0152	(0.657)
I_t			6.16×10^{-5}	(0.799)
Variance equation				
Constant	0.0547***	(0.000)	0.0534***	(0.000)
α_1	0.2622***	(0.000)	0.3499***	(0.000)
α_2	−0.0713	(0.164)	0.0396	(0.629)
β	0.6015***	(0.000)	0.5421***	(0.000)
Tue	−0.0659***	(0.000)	−0.0636***	(0.000)
Wed	−0.0523***	(0.000)	−0.0391***	(0.000)
Thu	−0.0459***	(0.000)	−0.0456***	(0.000)
Fri	−0.0503***	(0.000)	−0.0383***	(0.000)
$\lvert I_t \rvert$			−0.0006***	(0.000)
Diagnostics for standardized residuals				
Ljung-Box test		(0.263)		(0.106)
ARCH LM test		(0.515)		(0.678)
Log-likelihood	64.564		65.527	
Observations	599		599	

Notes ***, and ** indicate statistical significance at the one and five percent levels, respectively. Numbers in brackets are p-values. The Ljung–Box test denotes the probability of acceptance of the null hypothesis that the residuals have no autocorrelation. The ARCH LM test refers to the probability of acceptance of the null hypothesis that there is no ARCH in residuals
Source Author's calculation

We proceed to examine the impacts of auctions on the conditional mean and variance of the exchange rate change with Model (2). The coefficient on the CBM's net purchase in the conditional mean equation is positive but statistically insignificant. By contrast, its coefficient in the conditional variance equation is negative and statistically significant, implying that foreign exchange intervention by the CBM could reduce the volatility of the unofficial exchange rate change. However, its impact is quite modest. Using the estimates of Model (2) in Table 2, we can calculate the contemporaneous impact of the intervention on the conditional variance, $\delta_6 |I_t| / \sigma_t^2$. On average, the intervention accounts for 2.07 percent of the conditional variance. Such a result is similar to Edison et al. (2006).

4.4 Discussion

The empirical results indicate the auctions' modest impacts on the unofficial market rate. Nonetheless, their costs are not necessarily small. First, the CBM's sales of foreign exchange sometimes led to considerable outflows of international reserves, as described in Sect. 3. Second, banks may not use the auction as a facility to adjust their foreign exchange positions; rather, they arbitrage between the auction and the unofficial market. As shown in Fig. 3 in this section, the CBM's sales (purchases) of foreign exchange were mostly concentrated on the days when the official rate was lower (higher) than was the unofficial market rate.

Accordingly, the foreign exchange auctions should be regarded as a transitory arrangement at most until the interbank market develops to yield a stable market exchange rate. Retrieval of a market-based official exchange rate—the other function of the forex auction—may not justify its cost. The CBM does not necessarily have to retrieve the reference rate from the auctions; it is possible to label the prevailing unofficial market rate as the reference rate.

5 Concluding Remarks

Foreign exchange policy reform has achieved two highly visible outcomes. First, under the managed floating regime, exchange rates for various categories of foreign exchange have mostly been unified following the abolition of the "export-first" policy. Second, the CBM granted foreign exchange dealer licenses to private banks that offer customer dealing for private exporters and importers to exchange currencies officially. Moreover, the foreign exchange auction equips the CBM to obtain a market-based reference rate and an instrument to intervene in the forex market to smooth out exchange rate fluctuations.

Despite these developments, the bulk of foreign exchange transactions still appear to take place in the unofficial market. The turnover of banks' customer dealing has been notably small relative to private sector exports, implying prevalent currency deals outside the official market.

With regard to the linkage between the official and the unofficial markets, the empirical results suggest that the effects of the forex auctions in reducing the volatility of changes in the unofficial market rate are rather modest, despite the high costs in terms of loss of international reserves. The foreign exchange auctions should be recognized as a transitory arrangement until the interbank market for foreign exchange yields a stable exchange rate. However, the persistent unofficial market is one of the obstacles to the development of the interbank market. Chapter 6 will analyze the persistence of the unofficial market.

References

Baillie, R. T., & Bollerslev, T. (1989). The message in daily exchange rates: A conditional–variance tale. *Journal of Business and Economic Statistics, 7*(3), 297–305.

Baillie, R. T., & Osterberg, W. P. (1997). Why do central banks intervene? *Journal of International Money and Finance, 16*(6), 909–919.

Broto, C. (2013). The effectiveness of forex interventions in four Latin American countries. *Emerging Markets Review, 17*(C), 224–240.

Central Statistical Organization (various issues). *Selected Monthly Economic Indicators.* Nay Pyi Taw: Central Statistical Organization of the Ministry of National Planning and Economic Development.

Dominguez, K. M. (1998). Central bank intervention and exchange rate volatility. *Journal of International Money and Finance, 17*(1), 161–190.

Edison, H., Cashin, P., & Liang, H. (2006). Foreign exchange intervention and the Australian dollar: Has it mattered? *International Journal of Finance and Economics, 11*(2), 155–171.

IMF (International Monetary Fund). (2012). *Myanmar: Staff report for the 2011 Article IV consultation* (IMF country report 12/104). Washington, DC: International Monetary Fund.

IMF. (2013a). *Myanmar: 2013 Article IV consultation and first review under the staff-monitored program* (IMF Country Report No. 13/250). Washington, DC: International Monetary Fund.

IMF. (2013b). *Annual report on exchange arrangements and exchange restrictions 2013.* Washington, DC: International Monetary Fund.

IMF. (2014). *Myanmar: 2014 Article IV consultation. IMF Country Report No. 14/307.* Washington, DC: International Monetary Fund.

Japan External Trade Organization (JETRO). (2014). *Daily exchange rate survey.* Unpublished material. Yangon: JETRO Yangon Office.

Kubo, K. (2014). Foreign exchange market reform in Myanmar: Achievements and challenges. *Journal of Southeast Asian Economies, 31*(2), 210–224.

Kubo, K. (2017). Impacts of foreign exchange auctions on the informal market rate in Myanmar. *Global Economic Review, 46*(2), 189–202.

Chapter 6
Informal Currency Deals and New Official Customer Dealing: Who Chooses Which?

Abstract Normal trade export receipts—formerly labeled as "export earnings"—are still traded directly between private exporters and importers regardless of their legal uses. By using the original data taken from a survey of private firms, we examine which firm attributes are related to their uses of informal currency deals outside banks. The empirical results of probit regression show that firms' operational length—a proxy variable for habituation to the unofficial market—is not associated with the use of informal currency deals. On the other hand, larger firms tend to have used official customer dealing at banks, implying that secured and convenient transactions could be a competitive edge for banks to absorb informal currency deals.

Keywords Customer dealing · Informal currency deal · Hysteresis
Probit regression · Myanmar

1 Introduction

In Myanmar, although the reforms are paving the way for the bank-based forex market, informal currency deals outside banks remain widespread. Some informal currency deals are motivated by illegal uses of foreign exchange. For example, offshore account balances are used for smuggling; because authorized dealer banks do not make international payments for unofficial imports, smugglers raise foreign exchange outside banks and use informal money transfer operators for international payments. Informal currency deals for illegal purposes would persist unless the underlying illegal economic activities are eradicated.

A puzzling phenomenon is informal currency deals involving "export earnings" which are spent almost exclusively on legitimate uses. "Export earnings" are the revenues from official normal trade. For more than two decades, informal direct deals had been the sole means of currency exchange for "export earnings." Although authorized dealer banks started offering official customer dealing in July 2012, private exporters and importers continue to trade them outside banks. We question why informal deals of "export earnings" exhibit hysteresis.

K. Kubo, *Myanmar's Foreign Exchange Market*,
https://doi.org/10.1007/978-981-13-1789-7_6

There are several views that may explain hysteresis in Myanmar's forex market. One view is concerned with the development of informal market institutions. In general, when formal market institutions do not function well, informal market institutions develop. Private enforcement tools for contract execution become sophisticated in such a context. For example, a social network of firms offers a mechanism to sanction against firms reneging on informal contracts. Fafchamps (2016) argues that informal market institutions are not always replaced with newly established formal market institutions because the former has been embedded in a social context before the latter come in motion.

There are two other views about the hysteresis of informal deals involving "export earnings." One is the externality of the unofficial market; the more buyers and sellers remain in the unofficial market, the easier it will be for them to find dealing counterparties in it. The other is firms' habituation to informal currency deals. The informal market institution, market externality, and firms' habituation are not mutually exclusive.

Drawing on the data of an original survey of private exporters and importers, we attempt to identify the attributes of firms participating in informal deals involving "export earnings." A drawback of our empirical analysis is to view hysteresis narrowly in relation to firms' attributes, namely their habituation to informal direct deals. It is a limitation of our empirical model that it lacks a proxy variable capturing informal market institution development and positive externality.

The remainder of this chapter is structured as follows. Section 2 classifies informal currency deals into those motivated by illegal uses and the others motivated by official uses. Section 3 illustrates the differences between official customer dealing and informal direct deals involving "export earnings." Using the firm-level data, Sect. 4 describes the size distribution of the firms involved in "export earning" deals. We show that the currency deals concentrate in large firms. Section 5 presents an empirical analysis as to which firm attributes are associated with their choice of currency exchange mode. Section 6 summarizes the analysis.

2 Classification of Informal Currency Deals

Even in the period of the foreign exchange reform since 2011, there remain various patterns of informal currency deals. Some are motivated by illegal uses, others by official uses. Notably, offshore account balances and U.S. dollar notes (greenbacks) are traded unofficially.

First, informal deals of U.S. dollar notes for illegal portfolio investment are observable. Under the Foreign Exchange Management Regulation of 2014, domestic residents are permitted to buy and sell U.S. dollar notes at authorized dealers and money changers, but with a cap of USD 10,000 per person per day.[1] Dealing above the cap, which is illegal, are thus driven into the unofficial market.[2]

Second, currency exchange pertinent to cross-border trade with China and Thailand is usually held in the unofficial market. As described in Chap. 3, the authorities tolerate any forms of settlements for cross-border trade, which encourages firms to use Chinese yuan and Thai baht cash and the bank accounts in Chinese and Thai sides of the borders.[3] However, the Foreign Exchange Management Regulation does not allow Myanmar's authorized dealer banks to deal in such currencies.[4] As a result, exporters and importers who engage in cross-border trade sell and buy Chinese yuan and Thai baht cash and bank account balances between them. The uses and sources of Chinese yuan and Thai baht in cross-border trade are legal in relation to customs controls, but current international transactions in these currencies are illegal in relation to the Foreign Exchange Management Regulation.

The proportion of the cross-border trade in the private sector's official trade is far from negligible. Table 1 summarizes Myanmar's international trade by sector (state and private) and mode of trade (normal and border trade). For the private sector, border trade accounted for 38.6% of total exports in 2014/15. This proportion of currency exchange is extraneous to the official forex market.

Third, pervasive smuggling and mis-invoicing—illegal uses and sources of foreign exchange—accompany informal deals involving offshore account balances. The extent of smuggling and mis-invoicing are indicated in the significant discrepancies between Myanmar's trade statistics and those of trade partner countries (Chap. 4). Smugglers' demand for foreign exchange is not accommodated in the official market, as banks will not execute international payments without proper import documents. Smugglers, therefore, resort to *hundi* operators to buy offshore account balances and order international payments.

---

[1]The cap changed from time to time. The cap also applied to the withdrawal of U.S. dollar notes from foreign currency deposit (FCD) accounts. At the time of the sharp depreciation of the Myanmar kyat in June and July 2015, the CBM lowered the cap to USD 5,000 per account and further restricted withdrawals to twice a week per account.

[2]U.S. dollar notes are less likely to be used for current international transactions. In late 2015, the Myanma Foreign Trade Bank (MFTB) arbitrarily restricted outward international remittances for its depositors who had sufficient balances in U.S. dollars. As the bank faced a shortage in its nostro account balance in Singapore, it was unable to fully accommodate the orders for international payments. The MFTB treated the private banks that had foreign currency balances at the MFTB in the same way as other non-financial firm depositors and restricted their international payments from these accounts. Consequently, the premium on offshore account balances over U.S. dollar notes increased in the unofficial market. This incident suggests that U.S. dollar notes are not a substitute for offshore account balance for international payments.

[3]Technically, it is possible to order Chinese yuan- or Thai baht-denominated international money transfers at Myanmar's authorized dealer banks through costly double currency exchange from the Myanmar kyat to the U.S. dollar and from the U.S. dollar to the Chinese yuan or Thai baht. However, this is hardly practiced for border trade settlements.

[4]The authorities have given official permission for certain money changer counters to exchange kyat for Thai baht since May 2015.

Table 1 Foreign trade by sector and mode of trade, FY 2011–2015

	Sector	Trade mode	2011	2012	2013	2014	2015
Exports (USD mil.)	State	Normal	4,298	4,273	5,719	4,971	3,243
	State	Border	770	294	615	2,243	2,163
	Private	Normal	2,809	2,570	2,724	3,259	3,345
	Private	Border	1,259	1,839	2,146	2,050	2,386
	Total	Normal	7,107	6,843	8,443	8,231	6,588
	Total	Border	2,028	2,134	2,761	4,293	4,549
		Total exports	9,136	8,977	11,204	12,524	11,137
Imports (USD mil.)	State	Normal	2,066	1,330	2,462	2,723	2,516
	State	Border	363	188	92	32	31
	Private	Normal	5,629	6,500	9,470	11,416	11,457
	Private	Border	977	1,050	1,735	2,463	2,574
	Total	Normal	7,695	7,830	11,933	14,139	13,973
	Total	Border	1,340	1,239	1,827	2,494	2,605
		Total imports	9,035	9,069	13,760	16,633	16,578

Source Myanmar Ministry of Commerce website

Fourth, export receipts from official normal trade—formerly labeled "export earnings"—are used almost exclusively for official normal trade imports,[5] whereas they are traded in informal currency deals. The official market turnover data presented in Chap. 5 indicate that a considerable proportion of private exporters sell "export earnings" to private importers via informal currency deals.

3 Official Customer Dealing and Informal Direct Deals

For the subsequent analysis on firms' choices between (i) official customer dealing and (ii) informal direct deals, we illustrate the institutional differences between the two modes of currency exchange. After a brief review of the historical background of the "export earnings" trade, we consider how exchange rates and transaction costs are different in the two modes.

[5]"Export earning" FCDs may be held for portfolio investment. However, private banks did not pay interests on FCDs. State banks paid interests on FCDs at 1% per annum. Nonetheless, the bulk of FCDs at state banks were current deposits, implying that "export earning" FCDs were held for transaction purposes (Kubo and Set Aung 2017).

3.1 *Historical Background of "Export Earning" Deals*

Before private banks commenced international banking services, only state banks—the MFTB and the Myanma Investment and Commercial Bank (MICB)—provided such services.[6] While they offered international payment and settlement services, these state banks did not engage in customer dealing with private firms even for their official current international transactions. As a result, importers had to purchase "export earning" FCDs from exporters through direct deals outside the banks. Likewise, exporters had to sell "export earning" FCDs to importers when they needed to convert export revenues into the local currency.

The authorities tolerated informal direct deals between private exporters and importers via transfers of FCDs between residents' accounts. Both buyers and sellers had FCD accounts at these banks and exchanged FCDs for the kyat by using domestic account transfers. For the period from 1990 to 2011, such direct deals were, in principle, the only means of currency exchange for official normal trade.

Since the authorized dealer banks started customer dealing in July 2012, private exporters and importers have been able to sell and buy foreign exchange officially. Exporters receive international payments at a bank and sell the receipts to that bank for the local currency, while importers buy foreign currency at a bank and order international payments from that bank.[7]

Because the Foreign Exchange Management Regulation of 2014 restricts foreign exchange dealing to authorized dealer banks, direct deals of "export earning" FCDs between exporters and importers are illegal. Nonetheless, the authorities do not prohibit banks from FCD transfers between residents' accounts, which enable informal direct deals.

3.2 *Official versus Informal Deals of "Export Earnings"*

With regard to institutional differences between the two modes of currency exchange, we point out three factors: (1) regulations on official customer dealing, (2) differences between private and state banks, and (3) the settlement risk.

First, exchange rates in customer dealing at authorized dealer banks are subject to the control by the Central Bank of Myanmar (CBM). The CBM announces the official reference rate determined in the daily auctions and directs the buying and selling rates of authorized dealers and money changers within ±0.8% of the official reference rate. As shown in Chap. 5, the official reference rate sometimes deviated from the prevailing unofficial market rate by approximately four percent due to

[6] Another state bank, the Myanma Economic Bank, also offered international banking services on an irregular basis.

[7] Private banks active in international banking services include the Kanbawza Bank, Cooperative Bank, Ayerwaddy Bank, Asian Green Development Bank, Myanmar Apex Bank, and United Amara Bank.

the CBM's interventions.[8] Because of the gaps between the official reference and unofficial market rates, stringent implementation of this control would deter private firms from official customer dealing.

Nonetheless, the control on exchange rates appears to be enforced loosely. While private banks post buying and selling rates at their counters that are in line with the regulations, they often report to the CBM actual customer dealing exchange rates that do not conform to the prescribed band. This fact implies that the exchange rate control is not enforced stringently and does not always deter firms from banks.

Second, informal direct deals are more prevalent for FCDs in the state banks—the MFTB and MICB—than for those in the private banks. The state banks rarely traded foreign currency with private firms even after the reform. While the reasons are unclear, it might be because of their lack of ability to determine the buying and selling prices of foreign currency or to manage a currency position. Exporters who received international payments at these state banks, therefore, usually sold "export earnings" directly to importers. Accordingly, informal direct deals involving "export earnings" mostly refer to deals between depositors of the state banks, whereas official customer dealing refers to private banks' dealing.

From the viewpoint of firms, those that have opened FCD accounts at private banks are more likely to use customer dealing compared with the firms that have not opened such accounts. Those private firms inactive in seeking new facilities are more likely to continue with informal direct deals of FCDs via account transfers.

Third, a fundamental difference between customer dealing at banks and informal direct deals outside banks is the settlement risk. In official customer dealing, a dealing counterparty for firms is a bank whose solvency is monitored by the authorities. In informal direct deals, since laws do not ensure contract execution, the risk remains that the counterparty dishonors the deal.

Informal direct deals may yield favorable buying and selling rates compared with official customer dealing for the following two reasons. First, bank margins are absent in informal direct deals. Second, prevalent informal direct deals acquire positive externality, which lowers the transaction costs; the more firms that continue with informal direct deals, the easier it is for them to find counterparties. Furthermore, for authorized dealer banks, the primary source of foreign exchange to sell, apart from the Central Bank's forex auctions, is customer dealing with exporters; unless exporters sell export revenues to the banks, their foreign exchange liquidity is limited.

However, given the settlement risk, informal direct deals can be costly for two reasons. First, to mitigate the settlement risk, firms are likely to only trade FCDs with counterparties in relational links where private enforcement mechanism ensures contract execution. Under such conditions, the informal market could be segmented, and firms do not always get the most competitive rate in the market. Second, some firms rely on unofficial brokers who warrant execution of deals, but incur brokers' commissions on them. Whether informal direct deals yield more favorable rates than does official customer dealing would thus depend on relational links among individual buyers, sellers, and unofficial brokers.

---

[8] The gap between the overvalued official reference rate and the unofficial market rate for U.S. dollar notes reached 10% in June 2015.

4 Exporters and Importers in "Export Earning" Deals

Private exporters and importers of normal trade are the primary participants in informal direct deals involving "export earnings." This section first outlines the participants' profile using the firm-level trade data of the Myanmar Customs. It then illustrates the sample used in our empirical analysis.

4.1 *Overview of Private Exporters and Importers in Deals*

Table 2 shows the distribution of firm-level annual export and import values in the fiscal year 2014/15. The data covers only the normal trade of the private sector; it does not include either the trade of the state sector or the private sector's cross-border trade. The sum of normal trade exports of the private sector amounted to USD 3,123.1 million and the imports to USD 9,998.0 million. There are discrepancies between these values and the data in Table 1, perhaps due to differences in classification of normal and border trade.

Table 2 indicates that among 1,342 exporters and 6,671 importers, the private sector normal trade is concentrated in larger firms. With regard to exports, the largest 50% of firms accounted for 98.8% of total normal trade exports in the private sector, and the top 12% of firms—161 firms whose annual export was above USD 4 million—accounted for 79.4%. With regard to imports, likewise, the top 26% of importers accounted for 95.4% of total normal trade imports of the private sector, and the top 7% of importers—454 firms whose annual import exceeded USD 4 million—accounted for 76.4%.

There were a number of firms that engaged both in exports and imports. Among top 161 exporters whose annual exports exceeded USD 4 million, 85 firms made imports, and 76 firms did not. Moreover, among 85 firms that made both exports and imports, there were 14 firms whose import exceeded their export. By contrast, among the top 454 importers with greater than USD 4 million of annual import, there were only 73 firms that made export, whereas 381 firms did not. There were 18 firms whose export exceeded their import. At least two types of firms existed among those who undertook both export and import. One is export-oriented manufacturers, including garment factories[9] that imported intermediate goods and exported finished goods. The other is trading companies which often exported agricultural products and imported consumer goods.

[9]With regard to garment factories, they used the consignment production scheme wherein their foreign buyers provided intermediate materials on the buyers' accounts. Even in such a case, the consigned intermediate materials were recorded as the factories' imports by the Customs valuation.

Table 2 Operational size distribution of private exporters and importers, FY 2014

Category by annual export amount	Number of firms in category	Sum of export amount of firms in category (USD, million)	Share of export amount of firms in category to total export (%)	Number of sample firms in survey
(A) Exporters				
Above USD 4 million	161	2,480.7	79.4	21
Below USD 4 million, above USD 1.3 million	177	403.5	12.9	16
Below USD 1.3 million, above USD 0.5 million	173	145.0	4.6	16
Below USD 0.5 million, above USD 0.2 million	167	55.4	1.8	15
Export value missing				2
Subtotal	678	3,084.7	98.8	
Below USD 0.2 million	663	38.5	1.2	
Total	1,341	3,123.1	100.0	70
(B) Importers				
Above USD 4 million	454	7,640.5	76.4	45
Below USD 4 million, above USD 1.6 million	426	1,077.7	10.8	38
Below USD 1.6 million, above USD 0.9 million	450	537.8	5.4	38
Below USD 0.9 million, above USD 0.5 million	418	282.1	2.8	38
Import value missing				1
Subtotal	1,748	9,538.0	95.4	
Below USD 0.5 million	4,923	460.0	4.6	
Total	6,671	9,998.0	100.0	160

Source Myanmar Customs

From these figures, we emphasize two features of informal direct deals. First, while there were a certain number of firms that made both exports and imports, the bulk of firms, notably importers, relied on external sources for currency exchange. Second, private imports exceeded private exports by a large margin in terms of both the number of firms and the trade value. This implies that Myanmar's forex market in 2014/15 was a seller's market.

4.2 Data for Empirical Analysis

We conducted a survey of private exporters and importers in the period between August 2015 and February 2016 in Yangon, Myanmar. Yangon is the largest commercial city of the country, where the bulk of private exporters and importers are located. The population of the samples is private exporters and importers listed in the record of normal trade by the Myanmar Customs for the fiscal year 2014.

For the sampling of the survey, we sort the exporters and importers by their export/import values. Exporters (importers) below an annual export (import) value of USD 0.2 million (USD 0.5 million) are dropped from the sample. The remaining exporters and importers are stratified by export/import value into four categories housing approximately equal numbers of firms.

From each category, we collected sample firms using snowball sampling method; the rightmost column of Table 2 shows the number of sample firms. For exporters, we excluded firms whose imports exceeded their exports. Likewise, for importers, we did not include firms whose exports exceeded their imports. We collected answers to the structured questionnaire from 230 firms, comprising 70 exporters and 160 importers. Although our sample does not necessarily represent the population and the sample size is small, it still covers 10.3 (9.2)% of the entire population of private exporters (importers) above the thresholds.

5 Empirical Analysis

To shed light on the persistence of informal direct deals involving "export earnings," we analyze firms' choices between official customer dealing and informal direct deals. We first present some working hypotheses, review our data from the original survey, and proceed to the empirical analysis.

5.1 Hypotheses

Between the official customer dealing of banks and informal direct deals outside banks, some firms have kept away from the former, while others have tried them. Our question translates into which firm characteristics are associated with their preference to informal direct deals.

We derive three working hypotheses on firms' choice of currency exchange mode below. First, we consider the relationship between a firm's operational length and its use of informal direct deals. Informal direct deals had been the sole option for currency conversion for over two decades before authorized dealer banks started official customer dealing in July 2012. With more extended experience in the pre-reform period, they might be either habituated to or locked in informal deals. Moreover, they would have a broader dealing network and higher reputations in the informal interfirm-based forex market, which would bring them better deals outside banks. Thus, it is hypothesized that

Hypothesis 1:
Older firms are more likely to continue informal direct deals.

Second, from the viewpoint of the settlement risks in informal direct deals, firms who undertake larger currency deals are more likely to attach weight on safe financial transactions. Also, the transaction size is likely to be in proportion with a firm's annual export or import value. Hence, it is hypothesized that

Hypothesis 2:
Larger firms are more likely to use secured official customer dealing than smaller firms are.

Third, we need to control the influence of a firm's relationship with banks on their choice of currency exchange mode. Banks may offer better deals only to loyal and creditworthy customers. For banks, there can be economies of scope between customer dealing and banks' other operations. For instance, when an exporter sells "export earnings" to a bank, an opportunity is provided for the bank to acquire kyat deposits from the exporter. Thus, for exporters that maintain deposits at a bank, that bank may offer a better deal for currency exchange. With regard to importers, there are cases where creditworthy firms take loans from a bank and buy foreign currency from the same bank. Facilitating importers' foreign exchange cash flows can improve their profits, which adds to the bank's financial position as a creditor. In these cases, banks are likely to provide the loyal and creditworthy customers with favorable buying or selling rates.

As an index to measure the loyalty and creditworthiness of a firm, we consider bank loans. In general, private credit is extremely scarce in Myanmar[10]; credit advanced to the private sector as a percentage of gross domestic product (GDP) in 2012 was 10.2%, which was the lowest in Southeast Asia (IMF 2014). By assuming that a bank loan represents the loyalty and creditworthiness of a firm, it is hypothesized that

Hypothesis 3:
Banks are more likely to engage in customer dealing with firms taking loans from them.

Accordingly, we specify h_i, firm i's probability of using official customer dealing, as follows:

$$h_i = F(\alpha(trade\_value_i) + \beta(operation\_length_i) + \gamma(loan_i) + X_i\delta), \quad (1)$$

where *trade_value* is a firm's annual export or import amount, *operation_length* is a firm's years of operation, and *loan* is a dummy variable indicating that a firm is taking loans from banks. X is a vector of a firm's other attributes. We expect α, the

[10]See Turnell (2014) for the background on underdeveloped financial intermediation in Myanmar.

coefficient on a firm's export or import value, to be positive; β, the coefficient on a firm's operational length, to be negative; and γ, the coefficient on the dummy variable for a firm's taking bank loan, to be positive. δ is a vector of coefficients on control variables.

5.2 Survey Data

The survey collected information on firms' choices of currency exchange modes; their attributes, such as the size of export or import and operational length; and their relationship with banks. It should be noted that the data collection period was from August 2015 to February 2016, while the firms' export and import values were compiled from the Customs data for the fiscal year 2014.[11] In the survey, we differentiate between exporters and importers. For an exporter (importer), its trade value refers to its annual export (import) value in 2014, not the sum of its export and import.

A drawback of our survey is that we could not observe whether or not firms obtained more favorable exchange rates in informal direct deals than they did in official customer dealing. The survey interviewees, who were mostly accounting managers, did not have precise recall of the market exchange rates on the days of currency deals or were reluctant to disclose the dealing rates. In fact, apart from the data on firms' annual export and import values which were compiled from the official statistics, the survey mostly collected qualitative rather than quantitative information on firms' operation in international trade and currency exchange.

Table 3 summarizes the survey data. In this table, we divide firms into two groups: exporters (importers) that have never sold (purchased) foreign exchange to (from) banks, and those that have sold (purchased) foreign exchange to (from) banks at least once.

The survey results confirm the prevalence of informal direct deals. For exporters, 59% of the sample firms have never disposed of export receipts in official customer dealing. They rely exclusively on informal direct deals. Likewise, for importers, 53% of the sample firms have never obtained foreign currency in official customer dealing.

The summary of the survey results for exporters in the upper panel of Table 3 shows several notable differences between the two groups. First, the exporters that have never used official customer dealing tend to be smaller than those that have used them. The median of annual export value for the former group was USD 1.23 million, which is less than half that of the latter group. By contrast, there is no remarkable difference in the operation length between these two groups.

Second, exporters of beans and pulses—the main export commodity of the private sector—tend to have used informal direct deals; this is perhaps more to do with the limited options for international banking services in Myanmar. The primary desti-

[11]There were some firms that had exports in 2014 but ceased exports in 2015. In such a case, we dropped that firm from the sample.

Table 3 Summary of the survey data

(A) Exporters	Never sold export earnings to banks	Have sold export earnings to banks	Total
Number of firms	41	29	70
Continuous variable			
Export value (USD, mil., median)	1.23	2.84	1.82
Operation length (years, mean)	12.9	12.5	12.7
Age of owner (years, mean)	54.0	52.7	53.4
Dummy variable (1 = Yes; 0 = No, mean)			
FDI (Foreign ownership)	0.15	0.31	0.21
Industry–Garment	0.24	0.34	0.29
Industry–Beans	0.41	0.28	0.36
Have import business	0.27	0.34	0.30
Take loans from banks	0.51	0.41	0.47
Preference to foreign banks	0.76	0.59	0.69

(B) Importers	Never purchased export earnings from banks	Have purchased export earnings from banks	Total
Number of firms	84	76	160
Continuous variable			
Import value (USD, mil., median)	1.39	2.46	1.71
Operation length (years, mean)	13.0	13.4	13.2
Age of owner (years, mean)	50.8	50.4	50.6
Dummy variable (1 = Yes; 0 = No, mean)			
FDI (Foreign ownership)	0.04	0.04	0.04
Industry–industrial material	0.24	0.34	0.29
Industry–consumer goods	0.13	0.20	0.16
Have export business	0.12	0.14	0.13
Take loans from banks	0.29	0.54	0.41
Preference to foreign banks	0.58	0.64	0.61

Source Own survey

nation of beans exports has been India. Exporters to India often used MFTB and MICB for international settlements as these banks had correspondence agreements with an Indian bank that provided the settlement service in U.S. dollars which economized transaction costs; private banks have not obtained such agreements. However, as these state banks did not buy foreign exchange, most beans exporters sold their "export earnings" to importers directly via account transfers.[12]

Third, among the exporters that have never used official customer dealing, the proportion of firms that were not satisfied with Myanmar's local banks was relatively high compared with the group of firms that have used official customer dealing. The questionnaire asked whether a firm preferred foreign banks to local banks once a level playing field was created. At the time of the survey, foreign banks were restricted not to offer customer services to Myanmar's local firms. To the hypothetical question how they would act if customer dealing were available at foreign bank branches in Myanmar, 76% of the firms that have never used official customer dealing preferred foreign banks to local banks, whereas the proportion was 59% for the bank-using firms.

The summary of the survey results for importers in the lower panel of Table 3 indicates a notable difference from the results for exporters that bank loans are correlated with the importers' use of official customer dealing. Among importers that have never used customer dealing at banks, the proportion of firms taking bank loans was as low as 29%, while the corresponding figure for the customer-dealing user group was 54%.

It should be noted, however, that unlike in other countries where trade financing has developed, banks' sales of foreign exchange to importers were not necessarily linked to their lending to these importers in Myanmar. In other countries, banks often issue letters of credit (L/Cs) for importers on credit, which would yield a strong correlation between customer dealing and bank loans. This was not the case in Myanmar, at least at the time of the survey, as the banking regulations prohibited banks from lending using import cargoes as collateral. Banks usually required 100% margin or cover by the firm's deposits when issuing L/Cs for it. Rather, the fact that customer dealing was concentrated in the firms taking bank loans implies that the banks were selective of dealing counterparties.

Similar to the survey results for exporters, larger importers tended to have used customer dealing more than smaller ones did. The median of the annual import value of the firms that have never used official customer dealing was USD 1.39 million, which was considerably lower than that for the bank-using firms at USD 2.46 million. Regarding the operational length, there were no remarkable differences between the two groups.

5.3 Empirical Results

We analyze exporters and importers separately, as their behaviors in choosing currency exchange modes appear to be different.

---

[12]Alternatively, some exporters diverted international settlements to Singapore (Chap. 3), where international settlements to/from India were smoother than in Myanmar.

5.3.1 Exporters

We estimate the empirical model of Eq. (1) on firms' choice of currency exchange mode. The dependent variable is a dummy variable that takes the value of one if a firm has used official customer dealing at least once and is zero otherwise. The explanatory variables include the operational length and the annual export value. As for the operational length of firms, we use two specifications: one is the continuous variable of operational years, and the other is a dummy variable that takes the value of one if a firm was established after the foreign exchange market reform in 2011. We include two variables capturing a firm's relationship with banks. One is a dummy variable that takes the value of one if a firm took bank loans and is zero otherwise. The other is a dummy variable concerning a firm's preference of foreign banks to local banks.

Table 4 presents the regression results. In addition to probit models, we estimate ordinary least squares (OLS) models. All regressions show consistent results. First, the coefficient of the operational length is not statistically significant. This finding implies that older firms with longer track records of informal direct deals during the pre-reform period are not necessarily inclined to pursue informal direct deals.

Second, the coefficient of annual export value is positive and statistically significant. The probit models indicate that a rise in annual export value by USD 1 million will accompany a rise in the probability of the firm's use of official customer dealing by 1.5% points. This implies that larger firms are more likely to use official customer dealing.

Third, the coefficient of the dummy variable for taking bank loans is not statistically significant, whereas the coefficient of the dummy variable for exporters' preference of foreign banks is significant. This implies that exporters' preference overwhelmed banks' preference; as the market condition was a seller's market, exporters reserved more discretion relating to choices of dealing counterparties than banks did as buyers.

5.3.2 Importers

Table 5 presents the regression results for importers. Similar to the results for exporters, the coefficient of the operational length, either the continuous variable of operational years or the dummy variable for firms established since the reform, is not significant. The size of annual import is positively correlated with a firm's use of official customer dealing; the results of probit models indicate that a rise in the annual import by USD 1 million would lead to a rise in the probability of a firm's use of customer dealing by 1.6 to 1.7% points.

In contrast with the results for exporters, the coefficient of the dummy variable for taking bank loans is statistically significant at the 1% significance level. By taking a bank loan, the probability of an importer's use of official customer dealing increases by 24.5% points or more. On the other hand, the coefficient of the dummy variable for importers' preference for foreign banks is not statistically significant. These results

Table 4 Estimation result: Exporters

Dependent variable	(1) OLS	(2) OLS	(3) Probit	(4) Probit
Dummy variable: have used banks			Marginal effect	Marginal effect
Explanatory variables				
Operational length	0.0005		0.0003	
	(0.0091)		(0.0095)	
Dummy variable: firms established after reform		0.0813		0.0897
		(0.1640)		(0.1698)
Export value	0.0127***	0.0132***	0.0146**	0.0154**
	(0.0048)	(0.0047)	(0.0072)	(0.0074)
Dummy variable: taking bank loans	−0.0074	0.0278	0.0015	0.0389
	(0.1329)	(0.1386)	(0.1371)	(0.1446)
Dummy variable: industry–Beans	−0.2098*	−0.2098*	−0.2282*	−0.2213*
	(0.1154)	(0.1150)	(0.1190)	(0.1197)
Dummy variable: preferring foreign banks	−0.2513*	−0.2565*	−0.2705*	−0.2764*
	(0.1356)	(0.1376)	(0.1357)	(0.1378)
Constant	0.5888***	0.5574***		
	(0.1531)	(0.1336)		
Number of observations	68	68	68	68
R-squared	0.1112	0.1150		
Pseudo R-squared			0.0875	0.0907

Notes ***, **, and * indicate statistical significance at the one, five, and ten percent levels, respectively. Numbers in parentheses are standard errors of the regression coefficients
Source Own survey

as a whole are consistent with the interpretation that in the seller's market, banks sold foreign exchange only to those they selected.

5.4 Discussion

A key finding from the empirical analysis is that a firm's operational length is not associated with its use of informal direct deals. This implies that a firm's choice of currency exchange mode is not dependent on habituation. Alternatively, we can interpret the result as being consistent with the view that the exchange rates of informal direct deals were competitive. A limitation of our empirical study is that we cannot explicitly test the impacts of the informal market's institutional development or the positive externality (high liquidity) of the unofficial market. These factors cannot be well captured in our empirical model.

With regard to the empirical result that larger firms tend to have used official customer dealing, there are at least two interpretations. One is that firms tend to avoid the settlement risk for larger transactions. Another interpretation is that banks

Table 5 Estimation result: Importers

Dependent variable	(1) OLS	(2) OLS	(3) Probit	(4) Probit
Dummy variable: have used banks			Marginal effect	Marginal effect
Explanatory variables				
Operational length	−0.0009		−0.0016	
	(0.0041)		(0.0046)	
Dummy variable: firms established after reform		0.1195		0.1484
		(0.0943)		(0.1036)
Import value	0.0036**	0.0036**	0.0163***	0.0171**
	(0.0016)	(0.0016)	(0.0060)	(0.0062)
Dummy variable: taking bank loans	0.2405***	0.2564***	0.2436***	0.2658***
	(0.0794)	(0.0788)	(0.0817)	(0.0821)
Dummy variable: preferring foreign banks	0.0887	0.0959	0.1110	0.1173
	(0.0781)	(0.0783)	(0.0857)	(0.0865)
Constant	0.3045***	0.2589***		
	(0.0867)	(0.0747)		
Number of observations	159	159	159	159
R-squared	0.0994	0.1078		
Pseudo R-squared			0.1031	0.1112

Notes *** and ** indicate statistical significance at the one and five percent levels, respectively. Numbers in parentheses are standard errors of the regression coefficients
Source Own survey

offer better buying or selling rates to larger firms because of the lower transaction costs per value of currency deal. With our model specification, however, we cannot identify which of the two interpretations is more relevant.

The regression results for both exporters and importers imply a seller's market. Sellers' preference appears to have been more influential on currency exchange mode than the buyers' does. Indeed, the Myanmar kyat depreciated from around 1,000 kyats per U.S. dollar in December 2014 to 1,300 kyats in December 2016. Sellers might have reserved more discretion than buyers when choosing dealing counterparties.

Furthermore, firms' options for currency exchange were limited because of the underdevelopment of Myanmar's banking sector. Exporters to India favored MFTB and MICB for these banks' international banking networks which were at least once superior to those of the newly authorized dealer banks, whereas the international settlements at these state banks were combined with informal currency deals. Besides, while expectations were high for the foreign bank branches in Myanmar, their operations including international banking were heavily restricted. In this regard, lifting controls on foreign banks would be a policy option to nurture official customer dealing.

6 Concluding Remarks

The low turnover of banks' customer dealing (Chap. 5) indicates that informal direct deals involving "export earnings" are prevalent. Drawing on the original survey of private exporters and importers, we empirically investigated private firms' choice between the official and unofficial markets.

Our survey of 230 firms confirmed the prevalence of the informal direct deals involving "export earnings." For exporters, 59% of the sample firms have never disposed of export receipts in official customer dealing of banks. For importers, 53% of the sample firms have never obtained foreign exchange in official customer dealing. These firms relied exclusively on informal direct deals outside banks for their currency conversion.

The empirical results indicate that private firms' choice of currency exchange mode was not dependent on habituation. A firm's operational length was not correlated with its use of informal currency deals. In addition, larger firms tend to have used official customer dealing of authorized dealer banks, whereas smaller firms tend to have remained in informal direct deals outside banks. It implies that banks' secured financial transactions attracted firms who had larger currency deals. Finally, Myanmar's forex market during the survey period was a seller's market, which might be associated with the insignificant effect of the banking relationship on private exporters' choice of currency exchange mode.

The persistence of the unofficial market cannot be well explained by the attributes of individual firms. The empirical results are mostly consistent with the view that the exchange rates of informal direct deals were at least as competitive as those of the official customer dealing. However, it remains a task of future research to clarify sources of the persistence of the unofficial market.

Appendix: Bid–Ask Spread and Volatility in the Unofficial Forex Market

Informal currency deals may aggravate exchange rate fluctuations. The informal interfirm-based forex market is vulnerable to hoarding. When the Myanmar kyat depreciates against the U.S. dollar, anticipating further depreciation, sellers tend to hoard their foreign exchange, which in turn dries up market liquidity and leads to self-fulfilling kyat depreciation.

Fluctuations of the liquidity in the unofficial market can be inferred from the exchange rate spread. Figure 1 illustrates the bid–ask spread—the gap between the buying and selling rates—of the unofficial quotes for the U.S. dollar notes by leading money changers. The exchange rate quotations for U.S. dollar notes are widely circulated and are considered to be the benchmark for the entire unofficial forex market (IMF 2012). As shown in this figure, the spread is usually narrow, one kyat

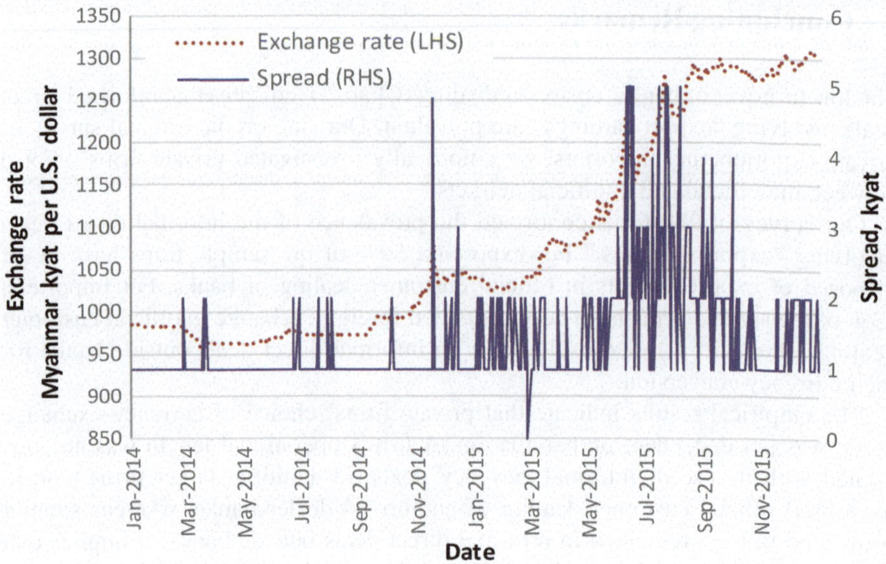

Fig. 1 Exchange rate and spread in the unofficial market, January 2, 2014–December 31, 2015. *Source* e-trade Myanmar

per U.S. dollar, while the exchange rate was between 950 and 1300 kyat per U.S. dollar.

Once the kyat depreciates or appreciates abruptly, however, the spread also widens to five kyats per U.S. dollar, which was the case in June and July 2015. A widening spread in turbulent times implies that finding trading counterparties is difficult. The situation would be similar or even worse for the deals of "export earnings" as they are between non-financial firms, whereas other dealing involve at least one money changer, who usually maintain liquidity in foreign assets. Market liquidity changes and exchange rate fluctuations due to hoarding are the concerns in the unofficial market.

Exchange rate fluctuations would be alleviated if currency deals were concentrated in authorized dealer banks. A concentration of currency deals ensures the banks to offer liquidity to the market, which would serve as a cushion against abrupt exchange rate changes. Also, banks are subject to the prudential regulation of their net open position and the supervision by the authorities, which prevents them from excessive hoarding.

References

Fafchamps, M. (2016). *Formal and informal market institutions: Embeddedness revisited*. Mimeo: Stanford University.

IMF (International Monetary Fund) (2012). Myanmar: staff report for the 2011 Article IV consultation. IMF country report 12/104. Washington, DC: International Monetary Fund.

IMF (2013). Myanmar: 2013 Article IV consultation and first review under the staff-monitored program. IMF Country Report No. 13/250. Washington, DC: International Monetary Fund.

IMF (2014). Myanmar: 2014 Article IV consultation. IMF Country Report No. 14/307. Washington, DC: International Monetary Fund.

Kubo, K., & Set Aung (2017). Dollarization in Myanmar? In K. Kubo. (Ed.), *Dollarization and de-dollarization in transitional economies of Southeast Asia* (pp. 105–129). Cham: Palgrave Macmillan.

Turnell, S. (2014). Banking and financial regulation and reform in Myanmar. *Journal of Southeast Asian Economies, 31*(2), 225–240.

Chapter 7
Concluding Chapter: Prospects for Modernizing the Foreign Exchange Market

Abstract We characterize Myanmar's forex market as the twofold prevalence and diversity of informal currency deals. Prevalence adds to the liquidity of the unofficial market and reinforces its competitiveness. Diverse informal currency deals include those embedded in the country's informal economic activities on which effective controls have not been implemented. Given these two features, lifting exchange restrictions would not suffice to eradicate the unofficial market. Resulting low liquidity of the official market runs counter to forex market modernization which requires a concentration of currency deals in authorized dealer banks. We present possible scenarios for raising the liquidity of the official forex market, with a focus on the roles of informal brokers and foreign bank branches.

Keywords Market liquidity · Forex market modernization · Informal broker
Foreign bank · Myanmar

1 Introduction

From the review of the evolution of Myanmar's forex market organization, we have characterized the forex market as the twofold prevalence and diversity of informal currency deals. The prevalent informal currency deals formed the interfirm-based forex market, which is in stark contrast to the bank-based forex market in emerging and industrialized countries. The conventional wisdom of the International Monetary Fund (IMF) (1998, 2003), that lifting exchange restrictions is sufficient to resolve informal currency deals, would not apply to Myanmar's interfirm-based forex market.

Drawing on key findings in the preceding chapters, we discuss strategies for modernizing the forex market in Myanmar. First, we summarize key findings about the structure of forex market. Second, we clarify the conditions for modernizing the forex market that are implicit in the bank-based forex market. Third, we present two specific scenarios toward forex market development. These scenarios focus on the roles of (i) informal brokers and (ii) foreign bank branches. Fourth, we list limitations of this book and present agendas for future research.

K. Kubo, *Myanmar's Foreign Exchange Market*,
https://doi.org/10.1007/978-981-13-1789-7_7

2 Key Findings and Implications

This book has explored the evolution of Myanmar's forex market organization and has shed light on the persistent informal currency deals. First, we summarize key findings of this book. We then draw implications from them for the evolution of the forex market.

2.1 *Key Findings*

By tracing its evolution from the start of the transition in 1988 up to 2011, we have confirmed two notable features of Myanmar's forex market organization: the prevalence and diversity of informal currency deals.

First, we describe the prevalence of informal currency deals in the private sector. The incomplete reform during the transition from a planned to a market-based economy in the late 1980s and early 1990s left intact both the overvalued official exchange rate and the central administration of foreign exchange allocation in the state sector. Liberalization of international trade in the private sector did not accompany either the surrender requirement[1] on private exporters or the foreign exchange allocation to private importers. Instead, the authorities let all currency deals in the private sector take their course outside banks. Consequently, two resource allocation systems stood side by side: the centralized foreign exchange allocation system of the state sector at the official exchange rate, and the unofficial forex market in the private sector at free market rates. In the private sector, bilateral trade of foreign exchange was the sole option for private exporters and importers, thus founding the informal interfirm-based forex market.

Second, we point out the diversity of informal currency deals that were rooted in extensive exchange restrictions. While the authorities turned blind eyes to informal currency deals, they imposed exhaustive administrative controls on international trade and international payments of the private sector; they tolerated residents' holding of foreign assets [e.g., foreign currency deposits (FCDs)] while restricting the outlet of foreign exchange from the country. The administrative controls included the restrictions on sources and uses of foreign exchange and the restrictions on international payments and settlements. These were intended to cope with the country's shortage of foreign exchange.

Exchange restrictions segmented the unofficial forex market further into deals of (i) official "export earnings," (ii) foreign exchange certificates, (iii) U.S. dollar cash notes, and (iv) unofficial offshore account balances. The segmentation caused multiple exchange rates in the private sector and distorted resource allocation. Furthermore, because the private firms circumvented the controls, informal economic

[1]To be precise, in the face of the enormous disparity between the official and parallel market exchange rates, the surrender requirement was abolished within two years from the liberalization of international trade in December 1988.

activities, such as smuggling and trade settlement diversion, spread out widely. The informal money transfer system further underpinned informal economic activities.

Despite the foreign exchange policy reform since 2011, the new official forex market has still underperformed the long-standing unofficial market. In the reform, the authorities abolished the peg and moved to a managed float using the daily foreign exchange auction that determines the official reference rate. The authorities mostly succeeded in exchange rate unification. They also granted foreign exchange dealer licenses to private banks. The newly licensed authorized dealer banks offer official customer dealing, which was absent in the pre-reform period. Furthermore, the authorities assist banks to undertake interdealer trading which complements the daily foreign exchange auction. Despite these efforts, the official market remains small. Our time series data analysis indicates the modest capacity of the authorities to smooth out fluctuations of the unofficial exchange rate.

Concerning persistent informal deals of "export earnings" between private exporters and importers in the post-exchange rate unification period, our empirical analysis indicates that firms' adherence to informal direct deals did not stem from their habituation. This implies the competitiveness of informal currency deals relative to official customer dealing.

2.2 *Implications of the Findings on the Evolution of the Forex Market*

The findings above are consistent with the proposition that Myanmar's unofficial market has reached a critical mass and acquired positive externality. Its high liquidity enables informal currency deals to outperform the newly launched official customer dealing by authorized dealer banks. Lifting exchange restrictions and installing official customer dealing would not necessarily eradicate the unofficial market.

Regarding persistence of informal currency deals, the interfirm-based forex market of Myanmar is in sharp contrast to the bank-based forex market in countries of ASEAN forerunners. In a bank-based forex market, informal currency deals are marginal, and they are for illegal uses and sources of foreign exchange. The transaction costs of informal deals would be high for several reasons: either they often involve cash transactions, there are risks of punishment by the authorities, or the market has low liquidity. In such a market, lifting exchange restrictions that legalizes the underlying uses of foreign exchange is sufficient to switch them to official customer dealing, as firms do not have incentives to continue costly transactions in the unofficial market. However, this is not the case for the informal interfirm-based forex market, as in Myanmar.

Besides informal currency deals for official uses, those for unofficial uses are also persistent. In particular, informal deals of offshore account balances are embedded in the informal economic activities on which effective controls have not been implemented, such as smuggling through land borders and the remittances of irregular status migrant workers. Strong complementarities exist between informal currency deals and informal economic activities, which are further underpinned by the sophisticated informal money transfer system. These complementarities are another source of the persistence of the unofficial forex market.

Even after the exchange rate unification, there is still a long way to go in formalizing the unofficial forex market in Myanmar.

3 Scenarios for Modernizing the Forex Market

We examine prospects for modernization of the forex market in Myanmar. Here, modernization refers to expanding the deals of financial derivatives, such as forward and swap contracts, which currently account for a major portion of currency deals in the ASEAN forerunner countries. After clarifying the conditions for modernization, we discuss two possible scenarios for forex market development in Myanmar.

3.1 Conditions for Modernizing the Forex Market

For either Myanmar or countries with an informal interfirm-based forex market where most foreign currency deals are not nested in banks, liberalizing banking operations is not a sufficient condition for modernizing the forex market. Our study proves that the conventional wisdom of foreign exchange policy reforms does not apply to Myanmar. Clarifying the implicit assumptions in the conventional wisdom, we elucidate three conditions for modernization of the forex market.

The first condition is the concentration of currency deals in dealer banks, which is the foundation of the bank-based forex market. The concentration of currency deals in dealer banks signifies high liquidity of the official market. Matching sale and purchase orders allow banks to manage their foreign exchange position efficiently and narrow the bid–ask spread. Furthermore, with concentrated order flows from customers, dealer banks can form predictions of exchange rate movements, which let these banks play as market makers, providing the market with liquidity.

The second is an interbank lending market wherein banks disclose their financial conditions and set credit lines with each other. Any currency deals involve settlements, and there is the settlement risk; a counterparty may fail to deliver payment. Without a credit line for a counterparty, a bank cannot engage in currency deals. Furthermore, financial derivatives put both parties under a longer-term debt obligation with each other. Interbank lending is indispensable for the interdealer trading of foreign exchange, especially financial derivatives.

Being subject to prudential regulations by the authorities, banks are better positioned to trade financial derivatives. As the authorities monitor their solvency, the hurdle is lower for banks to engage in financial transactions with each other. By contrast, it is not convenient for non-financial firms to trade financial derivatives between each other because it is costly for them to verify their solvency.

The third is a liquid money market with a benchmark yield curve. Banks usually set forward exchange rates based on the assumption of the interest rate parity condition between the assets denominated in different currencies. A benchmark yield curve for local currency-denominated assets is indispensable for banks to set forward exchange rates. Again, such a money market with a benchmark yield curve is almost absent in both Myanmar and many other developing countries. In Myanmar, while the authorities have commenced the auctions of Treasury Bills and central bank securities (deposit auction), the money market is still at a nascent stage.

A modern interbank forex market emerges in tandem with interbank lending and a liquid money market. Compared to the dissolution of the unofficial forex market toward concentrated currency deals in banks, establishing a sound interbank lending market and a liquid money market would be equally challenging.

3.2 *Two Scenarios for Modernizing the Forex Market*

We present two possible scenarios for fostering currency deals in banks in Myanmar. One scenario is concerned with informal brokers, and the other is concerned with foreign bank branches.

3.2.1 Informal Brokers and Merging Unofficial and Official Markets

As far as the unofficial market exhibits positive externality, forcing firms to move to official customer dealing via regulations can be a policy option to raise liquidity of the official market. Specific policy measures in this direction include the surrender requirement on exporters and the ban on transfers of FCDs between resident accounts. The ban on FCD transfers would prevent exporters from direct deals of "export earnings" with importers; exporters would have no option but to dispose of "export earnings" either by selling them to the bank in which they deposit or to use them for their own imports. In the context of Myanmar, however, a crackdown on informal currency deals by blocking FCD account transfers might backfire: it might stimulate smuggling among private firms as they try to circumvent the restriction.

The policy stance of the CBM has been accommodative, tolerating informal deals of "export earnings" via FCD account transfers. While this policy stance might preserve liquidity in the unofficial market and maintain its competitiveness, it avoids the risk of undermining the efficiency of currency deals in the private sector in the short term.

Another policy measure is to transform informal brokers to formal ones, addressing an institutional weakness of the interdealer forex market. Currently, interbank trade faces multi-faceted challenges, including its low liquidity and similar foreign exchange positions among dealer banks (all banks are mostly short of dollars). One particular challenge is that banks do not have sufficient order flows to form competitive quotes (e.g., narrow bid–ask spread). The resulting wider bid–ask spread deters interbank trade. In this context, informal brokers could serve as voice brokers to match interbank trade. They have experience in guiding the unofficial market. Ample order flows allow them to disseminate updated price information to banks. By officially mandating them to conduct brokerage between both banks and customers, interdealer trading can flourish. However, convincing them to become official brokers remains another challenge.[2]

3.2.2 Foreign Bank Branches

Another scenario for fostering currency deals in banks is to leverage foreign bank branches operating in Myanmar. The authorities issued banking licenses to nine foreign banks in October 2014,[3] for the first time since the former socialist government nationalized global banking majors operating in Myanmar in 1963.[4] Starting in April 2015, each newly licensed foreign bank has opened branches and started banking operations successively. However, the authorities have heavily restricted their operations. They are not allowed to engage in customer dealing with local non-financial firms. Their counterparties in foreign currency deals are restricted to foreign-invested firms and local banks.

Foreign bank branches can contribute to the development of the official forex market in two ways. First, the survey data in Chap. 6 showed that some local firms trusted foreign banks more than they did local banks. If restrictions on foreign bank branches are lifted to create a level playing field, more local firms are attracted to the official customer dealing. Moreover, foreign bank branches are equipped with better international banking networks, skills, and technologies than are local banks. International settlements and associated currency exchange at foreign bank branches would be more convenient, which adds to growth in official customer dealing.

Second, when foreign bank branches and local banks have complementary foreign exchange positions, interdealer trading between them is likely to grow. In emerging countries, foreign banks are often short of local currency liquidity, while local banks are short of foreign currency liquidity. Their complementary currency positions are conducive to interdealer trading. As the statistics on the forex market structure in Chap. 1 showed, in the ASEAN-4 forerunner countries, approximately 30 to 40 percent of forex market turnover was between local and foreign banks. By contrast, Myanmar's regulations on foreign bank branches restrict their local-currency banking

[2]The CBM reportedly communicated with informal brokers, but there has been no remarkable progress in converting them to official forex brokers.

[3]In the second round of foreign bank licensing, four more banks received licenses, including a bank from India in March 2016.

[4]Nationalized foreign bank branches include the Chartered Bank of India, Australia and China (the predecessor of Standard Chartered Bank) and the Hong Kong Shanghai Banking Corporation (HSBC) (Turnell 2009; Nehru 2015).

operations. The restrictions suppress their appetite for the local currency assets. Accordingly, lifting the restrictions on foreign bank branches in Myanmar would pave the way for interdealer trading which raises liquidity in the official market.

4 Agendas for Future Research

To wind up the analysis of this book, we list its limitations and present the agenda for future research.

First, while we presented indirect evidence supporting the existence of positive externality in the unofficial forex market, we did not prove it explicitly. In our argument, the difference between the informal interfirm-based and bank-based forex markets lies in the prevalence of informal currency deals. In the former, prevalent informal currency deals acquire positive externality, which translates to lower transaction costs of informal deals relative to official customer dealing. If we examine positive externality in the informal market explicitly, it is ideal to check whether the informal exchange rate of "export earning" FCDs lies within the bid–ask spread of the official customer dealing. However, it is not easy to collect precise information about informal currency deals. Besides, banks might adjust the exchange rates from one customer to another, which further complicates the comparison of exchange rates.

Another agenda for future research is the development of an interbank lending market and a money market. While our discussion in this book has centered on the forex market organization and emphasized the role of concentrated deals in banks, this is one of the conditions for forex market modernization. First, credit lines between dealer banks are indispensable for active interdealer trading. They are presumed for bank-based forex markets in emerging countries, but they are absent in Myanmar and other fragile states. Second, a liquid money market with a benchmark yield curve is essential for dealer banks to set forward exchange rates and swap rates. When we discuss forex market modernization in countries with the informal-market-based forex markets, such as in Myanmar and fragile states, nurturing interbank lending and money markets is an issue that is as important as is forex market organization reform.

References

IMF. (1999). *Exchange rate arrangements and currency convertibility: Developments and issues, World Economic and Financial Surveys*. Washington, DC: International Monetary Fund.

IMF. (2003). *Exchange arrangements and foreign exchange markets: Developments and issues, World Economic and Financial Surveys*. Washington, DC: International Monetary Fund.

Nehru, V. (2015). *Developing Myanmar's finance sector to support rapid, inclusive, and sustainable economic growth*. ADB economics working paper series No. 430. Manila: Asian Development Bank.
Turnell, S. (2009). *Fiery Dragon: Banks, moneylenders and microfinance in Burma*. Copenhagen: NIAS Press.

Index

K. Kubo, *Myanmar's Foreign Exchange Market*,
https://doi.org/10.1007/978-981-13-1789-7

The manufacturer's authorised representative in the EU is Springer Nature Customer Service Centre GmbH, Europaplatz 3, 69115 Heidelberg, Germany. If you have any concerns regarding our products, please contact ProductSafety@springernature.com

Printed and bound by CPI Group (UK) Ltd, Croydon, CR0 4YY
25/09/2026
02222904-0003